Political Liberalisation or Democratic Transition
African Perspectives

Mamadou Diouf

CODESRIA New Path Series 1/98

Political Liberalisation or Democratic Transition
African Perspectives

Typesetting : Sériane Camara

Acknowledgements: Carnegie Foundation (New York, USA) and UNESCO (Paris, France)

The Author

Mamadou Diouf is a historian, Professor of Modern and Contemporary History at University Cheikh Anta Diop (Dakar, Senegal).

He has collaborated and published in several research journals on the history of conquest, cultural and intellectual issues (19th-20th century) and the political and social problems of contemporary Africa. He has written *Kajoor au XIXe siècle, pouvoir ceddo et conquête coloniale*, 1990, Paris, Karthala; *Sénégal sous Abdou Diouf*, 1990, in collaboration with Momar C. Diop. He has also co-edited with Mahmood Mamdani *Academic Freedom in Africa*, 1994, Dakar, CODESRIA. At present he is Programme Officer, Research and Documentation in CODESRIA.

His current research subjects are the Formation of Urban Cultures in Senegal and the Indian and African Historiographies on Nationalism.

CONTENTS

Preface

This work is an attempt to outline a theme which has dominated economic and social studies on Africa over the past few years, i.e. the transition processes. The debate on the African continent is today characterized by what sounds like apocalyptic predictions. There is also a predominance of structural adjustment programmes stemming from the calculated supremacy of donors and the repeated failures of national policies. The key-words today are the (im)possibilities for Africa to achieve a triple demographic, economic and political, if not cultural or civilizational transition.

The aim of the study is not to fit into this type of reflection, but to attempt to carry out a thorough investigation in order to come up with a state of the art review, as well as a theoretical ordering of these processes. In so doing, we can clearly identify and give an account of the African situations and their dynamics, the actors and their strategies, within the framework of a general reflection on the democratization processes, which is not peculiar to the continent.

This state of the art review is coupled with a bibliography which is just a continuation of the work carried out by colleagues several years ago. And like the previous works that it draws upon, this one delineates a space for understanding the political developments in the transition from an authoritarian and/or dictatorial type of regime, to one that is more respectful of human rights and public liberty. The theoretical, practical and political African concerns should be at the heart of this space.

This study is an invitation to a reflection on the conditions for a possible African contribution to the theories and practices of the political transitions. As arbitrary as their choice might have been, the few non-African references included are works that have often informed the reading of African trajectories.

Introduction

In Africa, the beginning of the 1980s was a time of major political, economic and social upheavals. After nearly three decades of repressive, authoritarian regimes[1], African countries — reeling from the blows of structural adjustment and economic conditions — were more or less suddenly plunged into political reconstruction. There are many and diverging opinions as to the root causes of this political havoc, associated with violence, repression and an explosion of identity-based phenomena which gave rise to ethnic, religious and regional conflicts often preceded and accompanied by movements of political protest.

According to Huntington (1991), some observers — indeed the majority — point to the changes following the end of the Cold War and the defeat of the socialists (the fall of the Berlin Wall) as the source of the third wave of democratization. African elites were forced to rethink their modes of governance, since they had lost their strategic bargaining power in the global political arena. Furthermore, they had already lost all economic bargaining power and were faced with the dire urgency of trimming the fat from African governments since the flow of money for social pacification and bought allegiance was drying up[2].

On the other hand, certain commentators on the African political scene stress the decisive role of internal social movements sparked by political repression and human rights violations, and of acts of rebellion and resistance amplified by the economic crisis and of the states' own inefficiency. Although they recognize the importance of external factors — some tropical dictatorships were backed by Western governments — as early as 1985, a group of African researchers[3] began a study aimed at producing a different analysis of the diagnoses and solutions put forward by 'Développement accéléré en Afrique au Sud du Sahara', an action plan developed by the World Bank in 1981, and those proposed by the Lagos Charter of the OAU in 1980.

Based on their writings, it is difficult to distinguish Africans from foreign scholars as to the relative importance they grant internal and external factors. However, it is interesting to note that certain scholars who concentrate on the internal causes of democratic action movements cite causes which dismiss their potential to bring about change or a break with the past. They claim that political changes result from internal struggles between warring factions of the regimes in power, or that they are the legacy of a new president or a consequence of political liberalization. Despite their criticism of externalist theories, they have a negative outlook on the democratization movement, and do not question either neonationalism, patronage, or bribery. Indeed, they seem to see the movement as only another spin of the wheel of African elites (Bayart 1992). In the wake of the United Nations University study group which in 1985 was already interested in popular resistance to authoritarian regimes (it was indeed the subtitle of their publication) and the democratic movement, other authors[4], among them CODESRIA's Multinational Working Group on Social Movements and the Struggle for Democracy in Africa (1987), worked intensively to identify and analyse social and popular movements against political repression and human rights violations.

According to Bayart *et al.* (1992), 'grass-roots politics' or 'popular political action' are the main causes of the 'democratic explosion in Africa, sparked from within the sub-Saharan political systems themselves' (Bayart *et al.* 1992:17). This programme, which involves several African institutes, centres on the approach, the tools and the objects of study (mechanisms, actors, objectives) that can be used to account for the major upheaval which is completely transforming the economic, political, social and intellectual visage of African countries. The central concern which unites them is complete and objective explanation of what some call *democratic transition*, and what others, more suspicious in nature, term *political transition*.

Discussions of the nature of African political systems and the impact of the international system on its actions and reactions have dominated social science research on the African continent. These debates and controversies were long fueled by analyses of the impact of the entry of a subordinate Africa into the global marketplace (dependency theories), the issue of imperialism, neocolonialism in African states, the social class system, and the structures of patronage or repressive systems (Amin 1993)... The obsession with defining a central theme for intervention to promote development in the African context had the principal consequence of eliminating the holistic approach and bypassing certain issues such as democracy. This certainly explains African researchers' concentration on the problems of modernisation, development, and nation-building. In consequence, the great controversies that have shaken the political and academic world in Africa have rarely dealt with democracy, the democratization process or human rights except as a side issue. Despite its failures, however, this orientation has allowed us to better understand the mechanisms of patronage, (neo)nationalistic dynamics, authoritarian modes of governance, and figures of personal power...

Has the current crisis, which is also a crisis in our understanding of African situations, changed the epistemological approach to understanding reality in Africa? Despite a certain amount of innovation, this is a doubtful proposition. Examining civil society, culture and traditions, discourse on identity, irredentism and extremism of all kinds, in their complex,

3

contradictory and/or complementary relationships with democratization and institutional restructuring is insufficient if not to say imprecise. We currently seem to be headed down the same path towards the same errors, an idea which provoked the sarcasm of I. Shivji, who wrote about what he calls 'the prioritization of rights' and appealed to his readers to seriously rethink democracy instead of settling for a 'compradorial democracy'[5] (Shivji 1990a, 1990b).

The intensification of new social movements and political resistance to authoritarian totalization, the explosion of independent, self-regulated activity outside of, in opposition to, and/or removed from the state, the decline of the public sector, insecurity and privatization of certain previously state-run functions demand new discourses on democracy and civil society with new approaches and questions to define the new paradoxical situations. The urgent need to invent new tools for study is reflected in the dilemma produced by political conditions, virulent social movements and the extraordinary prevalence of violence in the African situation, be it public, private, or even domestic in nature.

The Current Situation

In this section, we will try to present the evolution of the political situations in Africa since 1989 as simply as possible. The watershed year which marked the beginning of many major changes was 1989. In particular, the first signs of resistance against authoritarianism and the first demands for democratic reform[6] became evident during this period.

The Geography of Transition

Table 1 depicts the political situation in Africa at the end of the 1980s. Table 2 should give the reader a clear idea of political change and the evolution of political regimes in Africa between 1992 and 1995. Even though we may question some of the criteria chosen here for some of the descriptions of African political regimes, the nomenclature used to organize the information in the table is useful. It helps us define parameters that allow us to measure the depth or superficiality of reform, its speed, and the degree of mobilization in the democratic movement and resistance in the ruling class.

As for the time of the democratic transition and the steps leading up to it, the dates given here are only approximates. The main road marks on the long road to democracy[7] are as follows: in 1989, the entire continent had only 'three tiny democratic countries', Mauritius, Botswana, and Gambia. Senegal started moving towards this group in 1974, when it authorized a limited multiple party system, but only joined it in 1981, when it adopted a complete multiple party system[8] (Holm 1989; Sall and Sallah 1992; Coulon 1988; Diop and Diouf 1990).

4

Table 1:
Human Rights Situation in Some African Countries

Human Rights Record	Autocracy	One-party Competitive*	Degree of Political contestation: Liberal Democracy
Severe and Widespread Violations	Chad, Somalia, Ethiopia, Liberia, Togo, Uganda, Zaïre, Sudan.		
Limited or Sporadic Violations	Angola, Benin, Burkina, Cameroon, Central African Republic, Congo, Gabon, Ghana, Guinea, Guinea-Bissau, Lesotho, Mali, Mauritania, Nigeria, Mozambique.	Burundi, Kenya, Côte d'Ivoire, Niger, Madagascar, Zambia, Rwanda, Sierra Leone, Malawi, Tanzania, Swaziland.	Zimbabwe.
Generally Free of Violations	Botswana, Gambia, Mauritius, Senegal.		Botswana, Gambia, Mauritius, Senegal.
TOTAL	**23**	**11**	**5**

Sources : US Department of State, *Country Reports on Human Rights Practices* for 1986 and 1987. Washington DC: Government Printing Office. Section 1, (a) to (f) for each country provided information on human rights; Section 3, information on the degree of acceptable political participation (Sandbrook 1988).

* includes monarchical systems with limited competitive elections.

Between 1990 and 1994, thirty-one (31) of the forty-one (41) countries which had never held a multi-party election organized this kind of election and three quarters of authoritarian African regimes sought renewal or reaffirmation of their power through electoral competition. In some cases, as in Benin, Congo, Madagascar, Mali and Niger, the authoritarian government was dismantled by a National Conference, and its defeat was confirmed by general, legislative and presidential elections. In other contexts, as in Cape Verde, Sao Tomé and Principe, Zambia, Malawi, the Central African Republic and Burundi, the re-establishment of a multi-party system and the calling of general elections had the same result: the defeat of the regime in power. In Namibia and South Africa, which are rather special cases, for the moment a very successful transition seems apparent and the situation seems to have been consolidated. These two groups are currently the most politically stable. Among the democratic countries of the first group, only the Gambia has dropped back into the category of 'ambiguous transitions' following the military coup in 1994. In the second group, aside from Burundi which is caught in the turmoil of bloody ethnic conflict, democratic promise is still in the air. This is the case in Niger, where despite the fact that President Mahamane Ousmane dissolved the National Assembly, the opposition has kept its majority in

5

recent elections. Other similar examples are Mali, where no solution has yet been found for Touareg irredentism, and Zambia, where President Chiluba declared a state of emergency and arrested the leaders of the opposition approximately eighteen months after his electoral victory. In all these countries, resistance by social actors, political parties and associations are working towards the consolidation of a democratic culture.

On the other hand, in countries such as Gabon, Côte d'Ivoire, Cameroon, Ghana, Angola, Mozambique, Guinea Bissau, Guinea, the Seychelles, Kenya, and Mauritania, although a multi-party system was re-established and general elections held, the incumbent regimes have remained in power. Other countries are either in ambiguous situations, such as Djibouti, Chad and Zaire, or in situations of 'democratization from above' (Bakary 1992a), or directed democracy. The only countries maintaining authoritarian rule are Libya, Sudan and Nigeria.

Conceptualization of Transition

Most of what has been written on democratic transition concerns Mediterranean Europe, Latin America, or certain Asian countries. African situations are usually treated as marginal. In general, authors limit themselves to testing the applicability of rules based on situations in other parts of the world. Their aim is usually to demonstrate the inherent differences in the African situation or to point it out as something quite abnormal.

This programme's primary objective is to achieve an independent analysis of transition in Africa, both insofar as the objects of study and the theoretical bases are concerned. In this perspective, it is indispensable to break with the way Africa has been negatively described by scholars. But it is equally true that this can only be made possible by a meticulous and rigorous approach to conceptualization which refuses the perception of African societies as dysfunctional, or at the very least, having a patho-logical mode of functioning where politics are concerned. We must lay down the empirical and theoretical groundwork for an African theory of democratic transition.

We are not proposing the creation of an academic ghetto. Rather, we are seeking for an African contribution to the general theory of democratic transition on a basis which is both empirical and theoretical. As such, this contribution should take its place in the international dialogue on the democratization process throughout the world.

6

Table 2: Political Regimes

Year	1992	1994	1995
Democratic Regimes	Cape-Verde , Benin, Senegal, Sao-Tomé-et-Principe, Namibia, Gambia, Botswana, Mauritius, Zambia.	Cape-Verde, Bénin, Senegal, Sao Tomé-et-Principe, Namibia, Gambia, Botswana, Niger, Mauritius, Congo, Zambia, Madagascar, Malawi, South Africa, Central African Republic.	Cape-Verde, Benin, Senegal, Sao Tomé-et-Principe, Namibia, Gambia, Botswana, Niger, Mauritius, Congo, Zambia, Madagascar, Malawi, South Africa, Central African Republic.
Democratic Transitions 1. Strong Commitment	Sierra Leone, Gabon, Mali, Congo, Côte d'Ivoire, Angola, Nigeria.		
Democratic Transitions 2. Moderate Commitment	Niger, South Africa, Lesotho, Madagascar, Mozambique, Rwanda, Tanzania, Burundi, Uganda.	Kenya, Guinea-Bissau, Tanzania, Madagascar, Mozambique, Eritrea, Côte d'Ivoire, Gabon, Uganda, Ghana, Mauritania, Lesotho, Zimbabwe.	Lesotho, Guinea-Bissau, Mozambique, Eritrea, Côte d'Ivoire, Ghana, Mauritania, Zimbabwe, Uganda, Tanzania.
Democratic Transitions 3. Ambiguous Situations	Mauritania, Ghana, Central African Republic, Guinea, Guinea-Bissau, Algeria, Burkina-Faso, Chad, Kenya, Equat. Guinea, Cameroon, Togo, Zaïre.	Djibouti, Lesotho, Swaziland, Guinea, Burkina-Faso, Chad, Sierra Leone, Togo, Zaïre, Gambia.	Djibouti, Zaïre, Chad, Gambia.
Directed Democracies	Morocco, Tunisia, Egypt, Zimbabwe.	Morocco, Tunisia, Egypt, Cameroon.	Morocco, Tunisia, Egypt, Cameroon, Burkina-Faso, Togo, Guinea, Swaziland.
Contested Sovereignties	Western Sahara, Liberia, Ethiopia, Somalia.	Western Sahara, Liberia, Algeria, Somalia, Angola, Rwanda, Burundi.	Western Sahara, Liberia, Algeria, Somalia, Angola, Rwanda, Burundi, Sierra Leone.
Authoritarian Regimes	Libya, Sudan, Malawi, Djibouti, Swaziland.	Libya, Soudan, Nigeria.	Libya, Soudan, Nigeria.

Sources: *Africa Demos*, 2, 2, 1992, 3, 4, 1994 and 3, 4, 1995; *Issue, A Quarterly Journal of Opinion*, 21, 1-22, 1993; *Afrique Contemporaine*, 158, 2ème trimestre, 1991, (Part 1) and 159, 3ème trimestre, 1991, (Part 2).

Theories of Transition

The starting point for this sort of theoretical project is the development of a common basis for reflection. From the outset, it is important to obtain a consensus on the definition of terms, but it is difficult to obtain a consensus concerning the concept on which the entire study centres-democracy itself. The various discussions and controversies are much too long to be taken up here. Different conceptions of democracy, however, tend to be divided into those based on institutional criteria and those which consider socio-economic equality and the presence of a democratic culture of social inclusion and participation as *sine qua non* conditions for a democratic society. But, it seems obvious, and this is the case in Africa, that in societies characterized by lack of resources and the hardships brought by structural adjustment programmes, the accent is much more on the economic aspects than on the institutional bulwarks of democracy.

Two elements can help us launch the debate on democracy. Firstly, we have noted that many observers are following the lead of Dahl (1971),[9] whose trail-breaking work, which has become a classic, centres on the existence of real competition and effective participation. These two notions form the basis for maximal participation and/or contestation on the part of social groups and individuals. By testing this theoretical basis, Bratton (1989) has been able to distinguish the following basic elements in the African situation: an electoral system, democratic political institutions, a transparent legislative system and independent courts, in order to determine whether or not a society is democratic. Sandbrook (1988:421) adds that:

> Liberal democracy... (is) defined as a political system characterized by regular and free elections in which politicians organized into parties compete to form the government, by the right of virtually all adults to vote, and by guarantee of a range of familiar political and civil rights.

According to Sandbrook, despite certain inherent limitations, the liberal democratic system does ensure certain rights, even to the underprivileged.

The second central concept in our reflection on democratization is the process by which people attempt to establish a mode of government which offers citizens the opportunity to contest political choices and participate effectively in the political world. It creates geographically defined institutions and behaviour in which pluralistic expression, electoral procedures and accountable government between elections should be solidly anchored.

In brief, when discussing democracy and democratization, it should be established that authority is always conditional, that it is subject to validation at regular intervals and that the relationship between the government and its subjects should be constitutionally determined. In the available literature on the subject, legitimate democratic power is always accountable and is associated with rules on independence, representation and pluralism.[10]

Secondly, it seems necessary to distinguish between democratization and political liberalization. This distinction is at the heart of every debate on the nature of political systems stemming from the 'second African independence' and the indecisiveness over how to describe certain situations of political transition. Chazan (1992:301) warns us of this confusion when she writes that, 'the recent wave of political change should not be confused with democratization', and Toulabor (1991:58) adds that these political changes should be interpreted as a simple 'transition towards more pluralistic political systems'. Finally, Lemarchand (1992a; 1992b) concludes, rather peremptorily, that liberalization in the guise of dismantling an authoritarian regime, can take place without democratization[1].

The best-known definition of liberalization is that of O'Donnell and Schmitter (1987:7) who describe it as:

> the process by which certain rights which protect both individuals and social groups from arbitrary or illegal acts committed by the state or by third parties are made effective.

This definition was adapted to the African situation by M. Bratton and N. van der Walle (1992:3). They posit that liberalisation,

> happens when a ruling elite grants previously denied civil or political rights, or enlarges the reach of the civil or political rights already enjoyed by the community.

In the African context, should we distinguish *democratization* and *liberalization*, the second of which was characterized by A. Bourgi as *institutional remodeling*, quite distinct from the democratic transition? Is liberalization the controlled concession of civil and political rights? Does the rate of these concessions depend only on the will of the 'powers that be'? In cases where the procedure is exclusively controlled by the regime, can we imagine this liberalization as a step towards democratization? Does democratization follow liberalization? Based on African experiences, can we better establish or contradict this distinction? Should we accept the sequential breakdown of the democratic transition process? Is it necessary to test the hypotheses of the authors quoted above on democratic transition? Among all these questions, one thing remains clear: it is absolutely essential, after the analysis of social movements, to test theories on the role of the elite in the creation of situations of liberalization and democratization.

In order to answer all these questions, we should first trace the historical movements of ruling or influential individuals in African societies, and identify the African elite(s). Their identification can be based on studies in Latin America, North America, and Southern, Western and Eastern Europe,[12] as well as on the following definition:

> We define elites as persons who are able, by virtue of their strategic positions in powerful organizations, to affect national political outcomes, regularly and substantially (Highley and Gunther 1992:8).

This ability to regularly and substantially influence decisions distinguishes the elite from other individuals or sectors of society. Also, there are two dimensions which are parallel and underlying and which can be measured either in terms of structural integration (formal and informal communications networks) or consensual surface (agreement among elites on formal and informal principles and codes of political conduct and institutional legitimacy). They also create a political situation which leans towards democratic consolidation, defined as a view of politics as bargaining rather than politics as war (Highley and Gunther 1992:10). From this definition, the following characteristics can be derived: relative inclusion of structural integration and consensus and recuperation of communication and influence networks. No individual or sector dominates another or enjoys exclusive control of the networks.

What results can be obtained by testing this conceptual framework in the African context? Although, in the Western context, we can easily agree to use the singular form *elite*, in Africa, for reasons stemming from the continent's history and the diversity of spaces and logics of legitimization and influence, we are forced to use the plural, especially until the confusion which establishes a sort of synonymy whereby elite = intellectuals = graduates of institutions using colonial languages (French, English, Portuguese) or classical Arabic (in North Africa)[13] only can be cleared up. This limitation to the social category making up educated people and their offspring reduces the elite only to those who control the public space and modern institutions.

This historical interpretation is an attempt at analysis based on the existence of a single geographical definition of authority and its public manifestation. As such, it is not convincing given the multitude of public spaces, legitimacies, images and idioms, powers and resources that have considerable impact on public behaviour and appearance, and given the heterogeneous elites that can as easily be competitors as partners. Due to the plurality and competition among elites, at every level of African political life we can witness patronage relationships, greed politics and co-optation, and reciprocal assimilation of elites or the 'reappropriation of the sphere of the contemporary state (...) by lineage heirs',[14] who are the 'intellectuals' of the people: clergy, prophets, healers, *malamoï*, marabouts and their ilk' (Bayart 1989:236).

Out of this diversity, various modes of representation arise which force the analyst to look beyond parliamentary representation and elections. This kind of representation and elections are the basis for the political elites' power to represent and act on behalf of the population. In fact, several authors have pointed out either the difference between real and official

Africa, or the high levels of activity outside the state and modern institutions, which demonstrates either withdrawal from the state or superficial adherence based on deference and consent. Social wheeling and dealing replaces the 'liturgies' of the state and a communal conscience is thereby consolidated to the point where it can make the bureaucracy bow to its will. Claudette Savonnet-Guyot had the following to say on the subject:

> It must be due to a lack of national consciousness that the state does not yet encounter any citizens in the public sphere. And it must be due to a lack of class consciousness that there is no competition in the economic sphere. But in the social sphere, the state meets competitors at every turn (lineages and villages, chieftainships and kingdoms of the past) who are well able to gather allies and loyalties, create and maintain networks of solidarity which, at best, are outside the state and, at worst, rise up against it (1986:11).

And so we see that African modes of representation often reproduce pre-colonial or colonial systems of inequality and domination.

The existing literature on this topic includes a great number of monographs, but little in the way of extensive theory, besides the work of O'Donnell and Schmitter. Different approaches can be distinguished among them: structuralist approaches which concentrate on social classes, macro-economic structures and insertion into the global economy; political/institutional approaches which stress internal political structures and individual strategies; and approaches based on social movements and civil society.

However, it would seem that the most decisive factors for understanding democratic transition processes result from analysis centred on internal movements. Indeed, authoritarian power structures often contain the seeds of their own destruction. It would be interesting to examine the division between reformers and conservatives within the ruling class, the army or economic groups as a means of observing the recycling or renewal process of the elites. Still, it is important to remember that neither the ruling class nor their replacements in the case of successful democratization,

> have allowed the contest for governance to slip beyond their control. In other words, the contest over political ascendancy in Africa takes place among the same groups of contestants: a very small elite (whether civilian or military) that generally favours political self-preservation over policies and political structures truly designed to benefit the disempowered majorities of most African countries (Schraeder 1994:85).

11

The debate over democratization and liberalization must be cleared before democratic transitions can be defined and classified. We can safely say that consensus is far from being achieved on the matters of definition and classification; however, O'Donnell and Schmitter's work (1987) is a reference in the matter of defining transition. They define transition as the interval following the reign of one regime and preceding the next. During this time, confrontations tend to focus on the nature of the political institutions to be established, the advantages that should be given to interested parties and the set-up and redistribution of public resources. The intensity of these confrontations tends to produce extremely fluid political rules; at least for a time, instability prevails. Therefore, the results are unpredictable and the outcome could be democratization, liberalization, or generalized violence and continuation of the authoritarian regime using repression to conserve power. R. Joseph (1973) tests the theories of the authors we have quoted by defining seven (7) models of transition in the African context. These were finally reduced to three (3) in the classifications established by the Africa Governance Programme of the Carter Center (CCAGP) (Table 2) which are:

1. A *phase of strong commitment:* of those countries which were strongly committed to democracy in 1992, Sierra Leone has entered a situation of contested sovereignty (violence/civil war) and Angola has ended the same situation less than a month ago, while Nigeria has become an authoritarian state and Côte d'Ivoire, a directed democracy (see Table 2).

2. A *phase of moderate commitment:* of those countries belonging to this category in 1992, only Rwanda and Burundi have not achieved democratization; these two countries have entered into a cycle of uncontrollable violence and genocidal brutality (see Table 2).

3. An *ambiguous situation:* in 1992, the majority of countries in transition fell into this category, which is one of strong resistance by the regime in power. While some of these countries such as Burkina Faso, Togo, Cameroon and Guinea are now in the category of directed democracies, others are now in phase 2, while the Central African Republic has become a democracy, and Algeria, a country of contested sovereignty (see Table 2).

These different situations demonstrate the unpredictability of transition processes. Table 2 offers interesting illustrations of regression, resistance and even offensive action by authoritarian regimes and the turning tides of opposition and social movements. For example, since 1992, the sudden contradictory movements in Angola, which was considered strongly committed to democratization, have not always indicated that the end of the civil war by an agreement supervised by the great powers would truly mark the beginning of a process of democratic transition. The return to

12

civil war after elections that were recognized as being fair and transparent illustrates the obvious reversibility of democratic renewal. It seemed for a time that a third force was emerging between the two principal factions in the civil war, the Movimento Popular de Libertâçâo de Angola (MPLA) and Uniâo Nacional para a Indepêndencia Total de Angola (UNITA), when the Americans seemed to distance themselves from their allies, UNITA, and the Catholic Church returned to the political arena which it had been forced to desert due to the threat of violence during the civil war. The return to war and UNITA's refusal to accept the election results underline the difficulty of ending situations of civil war. Perhaps the solution lies in power sharing, as demonstrated by the re-establishment of peace in Angola and the bloody excesses of Liberian warlords.

In Côte d'Ivoire, the way in which 'democratization from above' was carried out made it easy to foresee the victory of the Parti démocratique de la Côte d'Ivoire (PDCI) ultras in their battle for succession. This shows the fact that a commitment to democratization can be simply a political strategy for authoritarian African regimes. Succession was decided among the supporters of late President Houphouët-Boigny. And the construction of his successor's hegemony has already created a schism in the party in power, not to mention ethnic alliances and identity-based groups in which nationality has become a legal mechanism for exclusion. This is combined with a brutal return to repression and arrest of leaders of the opposition. Côte d'Ivoire is an illustration of the uncertainty of democratic transition. In the case of Sierra Leone, the impact of the civil war in Liberia and the regional policies of Nigeria have effectively put a halt to democratization, which goes to show the circumstantial character of political change and the decisive power of external circumstances. Rwanda is also an interesting case due to the following factors: ethnic confrontations; civil war; the incidents of the Arusha agreement; French military and 'humanitarian' interventions; many episodes of mediation; the role of the Church, which did not seem to follow perhaps for ethnic reasons the *aggiornamento* o f other African Churches which are now in the forefront of the crusade for the protection of human rights; genocide; and finally the victory of the Front patriotique rwandais (FPR) and the cycles of repression and departures and returns from exile. It is also interesting to note that outside of Rwanda and Burundi, the bloodiest transition phases leading to contested sovereignty, and characterized by the spread of violence and the rule of multiple warlords, took place in countries that were formerly under military dictatorship (Chad, Liberia, Somalia, Ethiopia).

The spectacular nature of these authoritarian excesses should not distract us from those situations where newly elected authorities attempt to recreate past authoritarian situations for their own profit. This is the case of

13

Chiluba (Zambia), who, eighteen (18) months after his election, declared a state of emergency and arrested several opposition leaders. It is also the case of Soglo (Benin), who, after dissolving the first Parliament resulting from the transition, managed to obtain a small majority in the new assembly thanks to a new party formed by his wife. Not to mention Mahamane Ousmane (Niger), who followed in the footsteps of Soglo, but lost his legislative election and decided to obstruct the opposition Prime Minister in his duties, creating institutional paralysis. Another example is Burundi, which held presidential and legislative elections after a charter of national unity was voted on and a multiple party system re-established. The opposition won, and in June 1993, a democratic system was established, despite hostility from a faction of the army. In October, a military coup put an end to the experiment and plunged the country into ethnic turbulence, massacres and the multiplication of armed militias which undertook a programme of ethnic cleansing in the neighborhoods and hillsides. Other countries such as Kenya, Cameroon, and Mauritania present situations that combine ethnic, military, and religious elements with outside interference, hence it is difficult to establish them in a clear-cut category under the *Quality of Democracy Index* (QDI)[15] of the Carter Center Africa Governance Program (CCAGP).

Other categories exist. The most interesting is the work of G. Martin (1993:6-7), who distinguishes the six (6) following phases of democratic transition:

1. A *change in regime through multiple party elections* followed by a relatively peaceful transfer of power from one segment of the elite to another. Two examples of countries falling under this category are Zambia and Cape Verde.

2. *A change in regime following a national conference.* This category is not defined in any precise way in the other categorizations we have mentioned. Martin's French origins probably influenced this choice of categorization which he divides into five (5) steps:

   • a coalition is formed by opposing segments of the elite who manage to organize a national conference and declare sovereignty;

   • a transition government is formed which seeks to obtain general consensus among the elite and progressively reduce the president's powers;

   • a declaration is made that the president does not hold power legitimately;

- the national conference is transformed into a transitional legislative assembly (High Council of the Republic), which elects a Prime Minister to supervise the transition; and

- a new constitution is adopted leading to presidential and legislative elections.

These conferences were described as *civilian coups d'état* by Togolese president, Gnassimbe Eyadéma. They have in common an irrepressible desire to cleanse the collective memory with the aim of purification (through rituals of confession and pardon) and the abolition of the past in order to lay down the foundations of pluralistic democracy. In the philosophical terms used by F. Eboussi Boulaga (1993), national conferences 'attempt to establish liberty as a way of life; they cannot avoid the obligation to create the conditions for a political economy of liberty'. They set up temporary institutions and create commissions to prepare a new constitution; their legitimacy does not proceed from the mode of designation of their participants. They are generally self-appointed, hence the disparities in their composition and the fierce battles over representativity, except in Benin. Their demands have always been viewed by the institutional opposition as shortcuts to power (Senegal and Côte d'Ivoire). And they have all introduced new players into the political arena.

The notion of civilian coup d'état used by Eyadema has been referred to with a lot of irony; yet it hits the nail on a situation which most analysts and political actors lose sight of completely: institutionalising African power notwithstanding the legal and legitimate fragility of their basic nature. If attention is effectively paid to the logic applied in the management of crisis, it appears that African personalised authorities are more interested in solving them constitutionally even where these constitutions are structured to suit the purposes of those ruling authority.

Contributions to the research network on 'Legal Successions and Democratic Transitions' (Diop and Diouf 1996) shed special light on the role of bureaucracies in ensuring institutional continuity, in a situation of leadership change, crisis or transition. This, despite the clientele and patronage. Such a situation contradicts all the approaches in terms of governance postulating the possibility (the capacity) to impose 'political conditions' as a result of institutionalisation deficits typical of African bureaucratic constructions. The role of Cameroonian bureaucracy in causing the failure of Ahidjo's return to power on the one hand (Sindjoun 1996), and, on the other, the arbitration of bureaucracy in favour of Henri Konan Bedie for the succession of Felix Houphouët-Boigny, to which the latter's last Prime Minister was aspiring, provide us with two excellent illustrations of the capacity of African bureaucracies to impose their 'institutional reading' (Bakary 1996).

3. *Negotiated transition* means that the regime in power keeps the upper hand in the transition process. The ruling class manages to preserve its power despite the fact that elections are held. The President of the Republic keeps his prerogatives and maintains to a great extent his ability to control the democratic movement by peaceful means. Côte d'Ivoire and Gabon portray this situation. Niandou Souley summed up this form of transition very well when he said that, 'the experiences of Gabon and Côte d'Ivoire are eloquent proof that democratization only served to legitimize the regimes of Houphouët-Boigny and Bongo'. Three steps have been identified:

- the regime bows to the opposition's demands for democracy by creating an open, multiple party system;

- it sets out an electoral schedule that does not give the opposition enough time to organize itself and present a credible alternative;

- these concessions are combined with far-reaching control over the state media and the administration so that the regime in power dominates the public debate.

4. *Democratization from above:* here, unlike negotiated transition, the regime is forced to make concessions due to social movements and riots. In this case, the model of transition is developed and controlled by the elite in power, usually a military elite. This is the case of Ghana, Burkina Faso and Mauritania.

5. *Authoritarian reaction:* the regime organizes state violence and begins a reign of terror, by setting-off ethnic conflicts in order to divide the opposition and intimidate the population. The climate of terror favours electoral victory for the regime, which goes on to use this victory to impose silence or exile on its opponents. This situation is exemplified by Cameroon and Kenya.

6. *Civil war or contested sovereignty: In* this case, no group is able to establish its authority over the whole of the territory or create a government recognized as legitimate either nationally or internationally. The obvious examples that come to mind are Somalia, Liberia, and Sierra Leone. Angola and Mozambique seem to have left this category thanks to their new agreements.

Does the situation in Africa allow us to develop other theoretical solutions or improve on those already developed through studies carried out in other parts of the world? How important is the role of the elites and their bargaining activities in the political transition process? Are the tragic events in Togo and Zaire indicative of their importance? Can we effectively compare African civil societies with those in Eastern Europe? It seems clear that reflections on the evolution of transitions in Africa will have to go beyond the approaches used in the past. The challenge we are faced with is how to go about it. With this in mind, we must not stop at examining the steps of transition, nor grant the elites either a causal or a messianic role. Instead, we should study them with respect to the forms of popular mobilization and the changing relations between the elites and the population.

Various scenarios should be considered in their synchronization (privatization of public violence, predation, militarization of extortion and commerce) and taking into account the structural adjustment policies which form the backdrop for all economic undertakings in Africa. Our contribution to the literature on transition by studying the movement from authoritarian cultures to democratic cultures should concentrate on the development or re-development of new political idioms and logics which form the basis for the continuing renewal of the political arena. By redefining new objects (riots, crowds and the language and discourses of African politics), we can rethink our ideas about political spaces, citizenship and politics, as well as popular and/or democratic participation.

The Steps of Transition

There are as yet no studies available which contain sufficient empirical data and adequate theoretical analysis of African situations. What are available tends to be either solid data presented as raw events, with few notable exceptions (Mamdani 1988, 1995; Oyugi *et al.* 1988; Mafeje 1988; Anyang'Nyong'o 1988; Ake 1992, 1993; Adam 1993), or theoretical constructs that seem to be inspired by nomenclature developed to describe Southern European, South-American or Eastern European[16] situations. The strong influence of these theories is visible in the phases chosen to represent the steps in the transition process. Two references that could form a basis for reflection are: the CCAGP's *QDI*, and another descriptive framework similar to the QDI, which was established by Bratton and van der Walle for a study by the *Global Coalition for Africa* (GCA/CMA) and the *Africa Leadership Forum* (ALF).

The QDI, which examines African political systems and regimes in transition as to their strength of commitment to democracy, could be an important starting point for our research. The QDI presents eight (8) phases of transition to democracy:

1. *Decay:* the government's decline affects vital sectors such as the safety and economic well-being of the population: the crisis slows economic growth and accentuates the unequal distribution of national resources. Political and financial scandals and electoral fraud are obvious signs of decay. The government is unable to ensure even minimum levels of efficiency and legitimacy. Its ability to resist or go on the offensive is undermined by

17

internal criticism and the promotion of democratic transition by its partners, particularly its Western partners.

2. *Mobilization:* energetic demands for meaningful political reform are taken up by various segments of the population (students, workers, religious groups and civil servants); emphasis is placed on a change of leadership, economic reform and a more democratic system.

3. *Decision* is a logical consequence of mobilization. The regime, faced with growing social pressure, decides to set up a pluralistic system. It institutionalizes certain basic elements of democratic procedure (responsible government, transparency, the legal state and electoral competition). This decision in favour of reform is, however, hindered by three obstacles: (a) it is a conjunctural decision; (b) the decisions do not solve procedural issues and they do not end the protests; and (c) the reforms proposed by the ruling elite must be approved by other political factions in order to ensure their success.

4. *Formulation:* the principles and details of reform are presented; procedures are established and the transition schedule must include the following elements: a new electoral code and constitutional reform or a completely new constitution.

5. *Electoral contestation* composed of the following elements: voters and parties are registered, an electoral campaign is held, the vote is taken and the results are announced this is a test of the transition. It should be remembered that procedures are sometimes abused by political groups or leaders in power for their own personal profit.

6. *Handover* is the orderly and peaceful transfer of power after an election.

7. *Legitimization* is ensured when the general consensus has been obtained on both the legitimacy of the government and the democratic system and their constitutionality. Opposition to specific policies such as economic reform or wage policies are not signs of mistrust of the democratic system.

8. *Consolidation* occurs when a democracy commands general respect for the constitution and more specifically, when a general consensus has been reached on the rules for handing over political power (*Africa Demos* 1992:11).

The consultants for the GCA/CMA and ALF prefer the term *crisis* over that of *decay*. They describe that phase as the deterioration of the economic crisis, civil agitation, general discontent and popular protest. Demands which were sectarian or corporate become general and the government's legitimacy is radically contested by ever-growing segments of society. The GCA categorization is interesting because it emphasizes not just the themes of protest, such as corruption, government incompetence, and human rights violations, but also the chain of government reactions to repeated protests.

The GCA/CMA and ALF consultants do not distinguish between phases 1 and 2 of the *Carter Center Africa Governance Program* (CCAGP). On the contrary, they believe there are two possible outcomes of the cycle of popular protest and government reactions: either the popular movement is put down by the government and the status quo continues, or the government is forced to make concessions and transition begins. At any rate, this phase determines the duration of the protest movement and allows us to determine the degree of organization and cohesion of both the protest groups and the ruling groups (*Africa Demos* 1992:13).

As for the transition phase itself (phase 3 for the CCAGP), it occurs when the government admits the failure of violent repression in 're-establishing order' and is forced to free prisoners and liberalize the political system by recognizing opposition groups and authorizing the publication of independent or partisan newspapers. As a result, the government is forced to negotiate with the opposition as the public sphere is opened up to more and more participants with increasingly divergent interests. If the opposition accepts the new rules of the game, stable rules will most likely be adopted. However, if protest continues despite concessions, transition will continue (*Africa Demos* 1992:13).

The third phase in the GCA/CMA and ALF's categories is that when each of the protagonists tries to force the other to make a maximum number of concessions, the opposition tries to further open the public sphere and those in power try to limit participation and protest in order to weaken their rivals. Ruling groups and the small number of organizations that come close enough to the level of the regime in power to negotiate with it appear during this phase. The process involves structured organizations which are not political parties, and it largely determines the success of transition, since one of its decisive steps is legal recognition of opposition political parties.

This step, which is not explicitly identified by the CCAGP, is interesting in that it forms the basis for the debate on the decisive role we lend to dissidence within the regime in the decision to speed up reform and establish transition. This dissidence is led by those segments of the ruling class who are most amenable to liberalization, or even democratization, of the judicial system and 'state journalism'.[17]

African researchers have devoted great amounts of talent and energy to this phase, which they study under the more general heading of social movements. They emphasize social phenomena as expressed in daily struggles both real and symbolic, through riots and state repression, through forms of resistance ingenious in their design and implementation, through false adherence and sudden outpourings of violence which defy all attempts at categorization and reject the theories that foreign scholars use in their attempts to apprehend political realities in Africa. The difference between approach and theory is meaningful. From the viewpoint of African researchers, this distance represents the will to emphasize movements and agents for change, but also the logic and the visible transformations of their actions. The image of the 'second independence' as a representation of this phase is probably the best illustration of the commitment of African intellectuals to identifying the elements of change, which can be compared to the great nationalist demonstrations which marked the end of the colonial period.

However, it should be noted that this mystique of social movements, which M. Mamdani (1995) calls the only indicator of the process of struggle for democracy, has also been contradicted in African political writings. After their positive characterization in the 1960s followed a period of doubt for some, or even outright hostility. Mamdani reacted to the contradictory nature of the movements by trying to establish different categories according to whether they are social movements, popular movements or democratic movements. But it was Ali El Kenz's remarkable work which best encapsulated the new tension between positive and negative poles within social movements. Based on the situation in Algeria, he cites the clairvoyance of CODESRIA's Algerian national working group which was already predicting great turmoil in Algeria as early as 1987 (El Kenz 1989). And in 1988, he adds:

> The Algerian state was torn apart under the staggering blow of a civil society disgusted by its corrupt, arrogant and incompetent leaders (El Kenz 1995:2).

This 'epistemological optimism' based on testing of working hypotheses and pertinent analysis has led Algerian researchers to envisage the creation of a 'Social Movement Monitoring Unit' (El Kenz 1995:2) expected to allow them to follow the development of economic, democratic and social modernity in Africa. It would now be possible to interpret the evolution of a 'society transparent to itself'. But, El Kenz (1995:3) continues,

> obeying an unexpected logic, the course of events was gradually drifting away from the mainstream, drawing the social movement into a completely new course. We had anticipated this course, but as an academic assumption, without much conviction, and hence without great effort of 'sociological imagination'.

20

In less than two years, between the June 1990 municipal elections and the 1992 legislative elections, there had been sweeping change. The actors and the stakes involved in the struggles moved from grounds which were paved with a long-standing experience in bureaucratic opposition, such as freedom of opinion and organization, equality and social and economic promotion, to the polymorphous spaces and quicksands of religion, of values and behaviours.

Underlying this rapid change is a strong and 'popular' social movement sweeping away all the old land marks: *Islamism*. The new 'heroes' are 'Cheikhs', 'Imams', and other 'Emirs'. While the new stakes are reduced to the application of the 'Sharia', civil law, especially as it relates to women, freedom of thought and knowledge and especially the areas of social and human sciences.

In this elegant passage by our Algerian colleague, we find all the ambivalence associated with interpretations of social movements in contemporary African societies. His prose evokes the perplexity of many African researchers.[18] The changes in direction that they may take reflect the nature of crises which are unexpected, rapid, widespread and violent. As Ali El Kenz (1995) remarks, they can:

sweep a country at a speed which only social scientists could dare to imagine. Which is why African scientists must now renew their approach to these phenomena, whose diachronic nature, so different from the 'cold science' of the North, can no longer be measured using the traditional instruments handed down to us by Western cultures.

This comment is key to understanding the absence of diachrony in the work of most African researchers and their unconcern for identifying the principal manifestations of social demands for democracy, except in the approach based on complex and contradictory social movements. Except for this approach, institutional reform and bureaucracy overshadow all other considerations.[19]

Of the last two steps, 'troubles/regression' and 'achievement' (GCA/CMA and ALF 1994:15-16), only the second corresponds to the final phase of consolidation defined by the CCAGP (1992). The first corresponds to a phase where the regime succeeds in stopping the transition process, or even turning it back, by reforming the balance of power in its favour. Unity in the ruling class and effective control of the army, the police, the justice system and the media are essential in order to turn the situation around.

The final phase, that of achievement, is the one which allows us to distinguish between democratic transition and political liberalization, since the second is an incomplete transition. This final step can include surprising reversals. The only addition made with respect to the category presented by the Carter Center is that, according to the GCA/CMA and ALF consultants, non partisan organizations able to enforce the electoral agreement are indispensable for the success of this final step in democratization.

Although this part of our study concentrates largely on the literature on transition developed in the Latin-American context at the end of the 1980s, there is another pole of comparison: Eastern Europe. According to Mbembe (1992:39), 'Contrary to what most seem to think, the downfall of authoritarianism in sub-Saharan Africa has very little to do with the events that took place in Eastern Europe in 1989-1990, even though both events obviously occurred during a global time that favoured liberalization'. Can Africa be included in that overall movement? If so, how and under what conditions?

Research Directions

The categories and reflections presented here demonstrate the importance of collecting and collating empirical data in order to develop theories that explain social phenomena. To illustrate this point, it is clear that there is a major difference between the categories established by the CCAGP and the GCA/CMA and those posited by G. Martin. This difference lies in the fact that the first two concentrate on institutional procedures while the latter concentrates on the social factors that lead to transition. In the first case, we have a tool for measuring democratization based on democratic standards and procedures, while in the second case, the emphasis is on the initiatives taken by actors and the negotiation process between different sectors of society.

In the approach adopted, methodological issues are central. Indeed, an extraordinary pressure is observed in the manner in which political science poses the question of how to view social transformation at the end of the twentieth century. Should we observe all the events and trajectories, including the complex entanglement of political, economic, social, linguistic, ethnic and regional motivations which, on the one hand, mobilise dissidence but also fortify promoters of coercive and repressive economy in their conviction that they are faced with the challenge of either remaining in power or disappearing and enduring social and public degradation.

The centrality of competition for all, in a context of scarcity and disintegration, of the exercise of public, private, domestic violence, require us to think of the changes taking place in African societies in terms of *itineraries, permanent recomposition of affiliations and genealogies* and thus go beyond typological approaches.

There are two essential reasons to the problems raised by typologies. It originates from a sort of classificational obsession which leads almost inevitably to dualistic and dichotomous proposals on the one hand. On the other, it stems from a confusion in statements on Africa which privilege social engineering, divinability, prediction and conditionalities.

It goes without saying that the possible research directions that could be taken on such a controversial subject are endless. By limiting ourselves to a few possibilities, we can ensure that our research programme will be much more precise and more complete. However, the following directions should be given careful consideration:

1. The problem of local/universal objects of study where transition is concerned raises a question: How can we account for both the unique characteristics of Africa and its universality as an experience and a source of theoretical constructs?

2. It is essential to identify the beginning and the end of the transition sequence in order to understand the dynamics at work in the processes still taking place. A certain amount of flexibility in defining objects of study could help us better understand the uncertainty of the process.

3. Do constitutional documents and the (re)introduction of institutions and judicial systems during the transition period reveal the shape of the coming regime, and if so, how? At this level of reflection, Mbembe's (1987) theories stating that democracy also entails the exclusion of certain segments of the population, at least temporarily, should not be ignored. He bases his argument on the facts of the French Revolution. A study of the revolution supports the idea that exclusion was not a result of the market ethic that coincided with the bourgeoisie's rise to power, but that bourgeois modernity was discriminatory in its redistribution of the fruits of progress. In order to disenfranchise the privileged communities of the Ancien Regime, it could only use mechanisms of exclusion. Does democracy have its origins in the historical contingencies of the French Revolution of 1789? And is it possible to find this type of exclusion in a context different from the liberal economic conjuncture? According to P. Blanquart (1992:101-102):

> Like grey matter, the public sphere consists of communications through which, unlike in symbolism, agreement is the result of a debate (consensus implies dissent), and not unanimous agreement with a pre-existing order or meaning. While exclusion is the product of competition in a uniform context (the indifference of economic liberalism); in principle, since communicative societies are based on diversity, they generally exclude no one, since each individual, no matter who he or she is, is in a position to enrich the society as a whole.

More thought should be given to the opposition between economic liberalism and democratization, between the excessive symbolism of national conferences and the creation of a democratic public sphere.

4. An examination of the role of international financial organizations and the political conditions laid down by foreign powers and their economic interests account for the external constraints on democratization in Africa.

5. Social movements should be studied in order to come to an understanding of their role in the democratization process. It seems that youth and student movements are often ignored. By paying them the attention they deserve, we can better comprehend the dynamics of opposition to and destruction of authoritarian powers in Africa. Religious issues are part of the same perspective. Several considerations should be noted under this heading:

- the return of religion to the public sphere is not only an Algerian phenomenon (we need only think of the spectacular Polish example);

- the intensity of this return is variable and affects Christian Churches (Kenya, Benin, Malawi, Zaire...), and cults (Zambia, Zaire...) as well as Islam (Algeria, Tunisia, Sudan, Egypt...) whose activities in sub-Saharan Africa seem to be much more conservative, although there are manifestations of some slight inclinations towards fundamentalism;

- is it accurate to interpret this return of religion as cultural renewal, since the superficial shows of religion by the post-colonial authoritarian states (their 'authenticity') had crushed community identity which it saw as unproductive for the nation? In that case, we should look beyond *stricto sensu* political commitments, since the excess of religion during the transition sequence is simply the expression of reconstruction of culture and identity, of which the intensity of ethno-tribal issues is also a manifestation; and

- are religious dictates in their African context (Christians, Muslims, cult followers, and local religions) one of the terms of the deconstruction of nationalistic ideology and the construction of a new order that coincides with political renewal and the liberalism of the SAPs?

Religious identities may be an expression of the social fragmentation that follows the destruction of authoritarian structures, or at least the reduction of their realm of influence. At any rate, the overlapping of political and religious powers, consecrated by national conferences, the recognition and subsequent abolition of the Islamic Salvation Front (FIS), the difficulties in managing the Tunisian Islamic movements, collusion between the army and Islamists in Sudan, and the inclination of part of the ruling class in Zambia to proclaim their country a 'Christian state', and finally, the strong religious overtones in

African political discourse, demonstrate the profound ideological changes underway on the continent.

This raises the question of the nature of the opposition, particularly the lay opposition, and whether or not it is committed to democracy. Can we accept J.-L. Schlegel's interpretation of M. de Certeau's well-known phrase, *'Quand la politique fléchit, la religion revient.'* (When politics fails us, religion returns.). Schlegel wrote (1992:173):

> We could interpret this idea positively: in times of hardship and struggle against the oppression or constraints of a totalitarian regime (totalitarian regimes being seen as either the ground zero of politics, or the epitome of politics), we have witnessed impressive returns to religion. But M. de Certeau most probably meant to criticize, and he was likely referring to democracies, periods of crisis in a democracy (economic and social crises are as likely as political crises to provoke the return of religion in its most doubtful and even its most dangerous forms).

Matters for Reflection

Two elements combine to bring the debate on democratization back to the heart of research on Africa: the African economic crisis and the attempts at reaching a solution, and the intensification of social movements in a context of social and economic deterioration. The challenge facing researchers seems to be how to reconcile the institutional approach favoured by donor and financial organizations in general with an approach much more grounded in the people's living conditions and the relations between structural adjustment policies, political and economic conditions for support, and the contradictory nature of specifically African phenomena in the flow of the global economy and global communications.

We do not hope to decide here which of these two perspectives is most apt to provide an intelligible explanation of African reality, but we will present arguments that legitimize the more explanatory character of the institutional approach. In the African context, it is difficult to explain democratic transition as a result of socio-economic constraints given the absence and/or relative unimportance of the bourgeoisie and the low rate of literacy and industrialization even when democratic protest questions the structuralist analysis — protest movements demand democracy. This is because a correlation between the magnitude of the crisis and the timing, content and speed of transition has yet to be firmly established. Consequently, the institutional approach seems to be the most functional, since on one hand it tackles the roots of political non-institutionalization in Africa: personal power and successionism, and mercenary, Mafia-inspired and corrupt reasoning, and on the other hand, it reveals the process by which political institutions are undermined at their bases, and allows us to make recommendations.

Economic Crisis and Governance

The economic crisis and the impact of SAPs and administrative, health, and education cuts, not to mention the end of spending on legitimization, have led to a transition whereby the state, which was the central player in economic development in the 1960s, has been disqualified due to the economic recuperation plans inaugurated towards the end of the 1970s.

The end result has been a questioning of governance or government management in Africa, which has rarely, if ever, been associated with the issue of democratization. For African leaders as well as for donor countries and international financial organizations, governance can be summed up as the establishment of a nation and its careful management by the government. From this standpoint, it is not important to pay particular attention to social demands, but rather to impose the will of the state, or the ruling class, as a priority. Civil society should be subordinate to the reason of state, whatever the means by which the ruling class accedes to power and whatever its claims to legitimacy. Given this theory of governance, African governments in the context of the African economic crisis have already lost the power of economic initiative through SAPs, and are now quite ostensibly in the process of losing their power of political initiative. 'Political conditions' and other commitments mentioned in the Baule speech are patent examples, whether or not they are sincere, and whether or not they are implemented at the end of the day.

The debate on SAPs and good governance only further complicates the controversies over democratisation since the ability of economic recovery policies to override social demands is far from negligible. Indeed, they tend to give free reign to the forces of the market. Mbembe (1994:277) describes this conflict as follows:

> transition to a market economy demands we set aside the 'political powers' of citizens and individuals, in other words, that they be disempowered under the terms of the duties and rights that allow individuals to have, not just duties and obligations, but also rights over the state — political rights which are exemplified by public services, for instance.

The principal question arising from this economic approach is whether the state, having lost the ability to redistribute wealth and define the political community and citizenship, loses its financial means, its administrative power, and its ability to regulate and arbitrate. It seems plausible that under these conditions, even for states in transition, structural adjustment programmes are an obstacle to the consolidation of democracy.

In his explanation of the reasons why the CODESRIA Democratic Governance Institute was founded, Thandika Mkandawire noted that: (a) approaches in terms of governance are linked to studies on Latin America. Their aims were to understand the failure of populist regimes and the institution of authoritarian regimes (which were not always military, but were always repressive) and to measure the responsibility of civil society in these situations. This work demonstrated the pertinence of the dissociation between *formal democracy* and *social democracy* and their implementation; (b) so far, studies on governance have been strongly influenced by their outside perspective. They are inspired by financing conditions and although their content varies according to the association that undertakes them, they remain solidly grounded in the imperatives of economic management. In this sense, reflections on governance are an international response to the African crisis. This orientation leads to the legitimization of central, Unitarian states (against ethnic, religious, or class movements) and favours administrative efficiency and the ability to effectively implement policies with disastrous social consequences (SAPs), even when faced with strenuous opposition (Mkandawire 1991:5).

The World Bank's criteria for measuring good governance include: *economic competence* (the government instruments and plans for development); *responsibility* of government members and civil servants in the use of public funds; the *transparency* of procedures and decisions about investments, markets and nominations; *dependability/predictability* of the government and its public institutions, which should never be capricious; *openness*, which is to say that information necessary for economic activities and development should circulate freely; and *legality*: governments and institutions should be subject to rules which are understood by all. Following this theory, the World Bank's support is determined by conditions in the following areas: public spending, civil service and semi-public organization reform programmes, support for the private sector, and freedom of information.

As we can see, democracy goes unmentioned and social problems can result from the application of these policies which are more concerned with ensuring *the governability of civil society,* than they are with the oft-mentioned *social dimension of structural adjustments.* The need for a legitimate, dependable state that can obtain obedience without excessive coercion, with no heed of freedom of assembly, freedom of speech, or a legal system and legal practices that respect human rights have become the rule in political restructuring operations in Africa.

27

Between yesterday's question of how can African societies govern themselves to the contemporary question of what is the best form of government, Africa's destiny will be played out under pressures from external constraints and internal social demands with very violent means of expression, and the repressive means by which they would be contained. Our challenge is to produce a political economy of transition allowing us to reconcile democratization, fiscal policy and social demands. So far, the SAPs have not made this a reality.

Social Movements

In Africa, the end of the 1980s was marked by the intensification of popular struggle and increasingly violent protest against authoritarian systems. Since then, these movements have only grown more radical. In the streets of African capitals and other large cities, new social players have appeared, and new mobilization procedures and new ideological themes have arisen, with democracy chief among them. The socio-economic context which is largely the result of the operations of structural adjustment programmes have served as a backdrop and often as a detonator for crises which have shaken almost every African regime since the end of the 1980s.

The institution of democratic process and pluralism in Africa contains elements that are common to the entire continent: economic dissatisfaction, the legitimacy crisis and so on, as in Benin, Zaire, the Congo and Zambia, which are the clearest examples of economic bankruptcy. In order to ground our theory, we must necessarily establish a chronology and some of the principal characteristics, while avoiding any preconceived ideas on their content or their dynamics.

These movements are essentially urban movements led by unemployed or educated youth, teachers and students, journalists and lawyers, human rights movements, laid-off workers, etc., 'who have often held an important place in the struggle for multiple party systems and human rights' (*Afrique contemporaine* 1991a). In another analysis of the subject by *Afrique Contemporaine*, there is a chronology of social and political demonstrations in Africa. Although the authors' interpretations of events are overly representative of situations in French-speaking Africa (particularly Benin and Togo), the analysis seems to offer a precise and empirical tableau of social crises in various African countries. It also offers very precise indications of who is involved in protest movements and restructuring authoritarian order (*Afrique contemporaine* 1991b).

When we examine other French-speaking areas, students and teachers seemed to have played a greater role (Côte d'Ivoire, Niger, Mali); in some cases, the civil service was particularly active (Madagascar). In others, there was dissension within the elite (Kenya) or an episode of civil war followed by solutions for peace (Rwanda, Angola, Mozambique). Also, in many English-speaking African countries, trade unions seemed to play an important role (Zambia, Malawi), along with the players identified in the other countries.

To the empirical data gathered in *Afrique Contemporaine*'s collection, we could add the more theoretical approach taken in M. Bratton and N. van der Walle's (1992:27-56) two-fold article. They present a table showing popular demonstrations in fifteen (15) African countries over one year (November 1989-November 1990) using variables such as the roles of students, civil servants, unions, churches, and defection among members of the ruling elite.

This situation, like 'the end of salaries as bribes for the general public and their replacement by occasional payments, transform the basis for rights, transfers and duties that were established in the past, and hence the very definition of post-colonial citizenship' (Mbembe 1994:283) and has profoundly changed individuals and communities' relations with the state and public office holders.

The deterioration of the public sphere, which is a result of both the means of appropriation used by the ruling class, and their creation of a separate public sphere with its own points of reference, has had disastrous consequences on the territory they control. By seeking to exclude others, it ends up excluding itself. The fragmentation and circumscription of areas of discrimination causes a return to violence, which is the criminalization of political dissent. This type of political activity, which C. Aké identified in countries under authoritarian regimes, has become an essential element in the process of loosening the hold of authoritarian regimes in Africa.

The mechanisms of exclusion operating during the establishment of a nationalistic ideology have globally impacted women and youths, both for political reasons and due to 'traditional socialization'. These procedures have lent a unique character to the political activities of women and youths in the current phase. The fact that those in power refuse to grant recognition to independent organizations while reviving formal organizations has led young people, and especially women, to enter the informal sector and create small organizations of a much more democratic and community-oriented nature. According to Tripp (1994:111-112), women have adopted these practices because:

> Women's role in the informal sector and private enterprise has been in a large measure determined by the fact that women have been less tied to the formal economy than men and have no access to jobs in the formal wage sector due to lack of education and discriminatory hiring practices...

As women, they generally have not had access to patronage and personal networks tied to the state and instead are part of the emerging bourgeoisie in Africa that is not based on extracting and diverting state resources.

And this is how ideas of representation and pluralistic leadership were originally supplanted by Unitarian ideas of submission to a single central authority.

The return, or at least the reactivation of representations of the invisible as witnessed by P. Geshiere (1995), the return to migration, the coexistence of central authority with other, more or less independent centres of power, the end of the monopoly on legitimate use of violence, and the multi- plication of closely watched areas where small groups confront each other on the basis of illicit practices and xenophobic identities, have destroyed the basis for territory and national citizenship. The result is a proliferation of social spaces which totally escape the authority of the state, and of religious, ethnic and economic representations that serve the political and social strategies of social movements and popular movements (Mamdani and Wamba-dia-Wamba 1995). The process of independent organization of social groups, and the reactivation of certain social groups, such as funeral societies in Zimbabwe and Côte d'Ivoire which originated during the colonial period as a response to the process of proletarianization, are gaining ground in the climate of insecurity caused by structural adjustment programmes. In Nigeria, the extraordinary virulence of the *area boys*[20] and *yan daba* (Simone and Pieterse 1993:41-49), or *langa* in the province of Western Cape, in South Africa, brings vital and often criminal focus to the historical and territorial dimensions of representation and citizenship.

Recourse to violence, as symbolic purification by fire; the destruction of places and monuments of post-colonial munificence, as though seeking to efface its territorial markers, are common elements of the principally youth-led social movements. The uprooting of post-colonial legitimacies can be seen in several events: the riots organized by students in Mali (April 5, 1993) (Diarrah 1993), the removal of certain neighborhoods in Lagos and certain Nigerian cities from the authority of the administration and politicians, unless they have the support of the *area boys*, and the vital role played by the disaffected youth in the armed struggles in Liberia and Sierra Leone (Richards 1993:4-5). The organization of violent demonstrations seems to owe a lot to the images of the modern visual media, including riots in the South African townships and occupied territories in Gaza and the West Bank, and films such as *Rambo* and *Terminator*.

The generalization of violence, even domestic violence, should incite us to re-examine the issue of the army and the military in the democratization process.

The Army and the Military

What first springs to mind when we address the issue of the military in the democratic transition process is either its absence from the debate, or its questionable treatment by democratic forces. According to some observers, the military's attitude determines on whether or not it is possible to have trouble-free democratic transition (Benin, Zambia, Mali). The challenge is thus: to impose neutrality or neutralize the army. But is it necessary, as in Latin America, to conclude that the presence of armies on the political stage is a symptom of the pathological nature of civil society. And is it crucial to strike a compromise with the military in order to avoid a military regime? Or should we envisage total abolition of armies in Africa in hopes of putting authoritarianism behind us forever? In most situations, the military has been decried by democratic forces, and in every case, they have been either against democratic and/or civilian control of the army (Togo, Côte d'Ivoire, Niger, Zaire, Madagascar) or neutral.

On the subject of armies in Africa, it seems apparent that the essential issue for the democratic movement is how to reconcile the global political transition processes with military procedures. If we hope to place the military under the authority of civilian powers, three problems must first be resolved, and these are: the army's fiscal management, especially in the context of structural adjustment, ensuring dependable military expertise, and greater stability and unity. The second factor is very important, since African armies, which are maintained at a high cost, often collapse when faced with less conventional tactics of rebels (Chad, and the latest performance by the Ethiopian army). There seems to be some degree of contradiction between the political hegemony of the military and their weakness as a fighting force.

Our research project will examine several new issues, while keeping an attentive eye on the conclusions of the Multinational Working Group on Military and Militarism in Africa:

1. In most cases, military leadership in Africa has close ties to civilian leadership. These ties can lead to the development of ethnically homogeneous troops used as bodyguards (Togo), or mercenary guards (Zaire), or even over-armed battalions belonging to the same army as the autocrat (the Madagascan president's marine corps). Could this collusion between politicians and the military (they may belong to the same ruling group) be the cause of civilian ignorance of the military institution and the military's absence from intellectual and particularly academic debate? Is

31

this situation of mutual ignorance the result of a deliberate strategy undertaken by military and political leaders?

2. We can distinguish between military institutions and military regimes by attempting to introduce the methods and dynamics of military change. How and why does the lack of proper institutionalization of the military and law-enforcement agencies affect the democratic transition process? This distinction and its effects on the democratisation process should not overshadow the fact that non-institutional or informal elements of force and constraint are also at work in post-colonial Africa. And if war is a form of social and political management, should we not consider Chad, Southern Sudan, Mozambique, the Touaregs on the Saharan fringes of Mali and the Niger, more recently, Somalia and Liberia, and formerly, Ethiopia and Angola, as reasons to re-evaluate categories such as the military and militarization in Africa? In several countries, the military has started riots (Zaire, Liberia, Chad, Côte d'Ivoire). In other situations, the heads of certain political factions are also military entrepreneurs (Chad, Somalia, Ethiopia, Angola). In peaceable, civilian countries, how can we explain the organization of constraint which is not necessarily associated with military regimes alone? What are the sources of constraint, the methods of surveillance and punishment, and what is their impact on the country's productivity, its politics and its social relations? These issues, which are too often neglected by all but human rights advocacy groups, should be mandatory in research on transition. They are vital to our understanding of the role of the police in the political transition process and also in the legal succession process. And the privatization of public forces for profit raises the question of law enforcement management in the transition context. It appears self-evident that political transition must be preceded by a change in the administration of violence.

3. Can military structures be democratized? How can the democratic movement answer this question? From this perspective, how can one deal with ethnically homogeneous military structures (Togo), or armies serving as government bodyguards (Zaire), or mercenary militia? Should democracy be envisaged in the form of demilitarization and/or demobilization? What can be done with demobilized troops?

4. What is the impact of the fragmentation of military structures, the leadership problem (based on military or political expertise, charisma), hierarchical relations in the military and stratification of society in general on the democratization and transition process and how can we follow their evolution?

It is obvious that the questions presented above are not exhaustive and that we should not lose sight of individual national situations. For example, in some countries (Burkina Faso), in an attempt to end the division between the military and civilians, non-military armed groups were created (militia), while in other countries (Nigeria) it is believed that military issues should remain confidential, that they can only be understood by military experts and that they should therefore have exclusive rights to this domain. And how can democracy be established in countries where personal control (privatization) of the army (Togo, Zaire) has stripped it of its national character?

Administration

After being travestied by authoritarian and mercenary reasoning, public administration is losing its hegemony under the combined influence of SAPs, with the slow erosion of its structures and subversion of its procedures by identity politics, party politics and nepotism. African public administration has been hit with the full force of the economic crisis, personnel cuts, the privatization of certain government functions or the appointment of expatriate managers — much as in colonial concessions — which creates immunity for certain sectors. Administration is increasingly becoming a prerogative if not a favour. In this sense, public administration has become an essential locus of transition to democracy.

The geography of public administration and its ability to avoid political combats while ensuring the continuing efficiency of the public service seems to be related to its accountability, to the predictability of its decisions and its affirmation of administrative, constitutional, and legislative regulations which ensure an even spread of power among various branches of the state.

The continued weakening of the state and the intensified social competition within and among groups which are more and more independent from the government's authority reflect an increasingly radical refusal of the integrating model — SAPs included — of the elite. This is the case of Nigerian merchants (Gregoire 1993), Algerian and Tunisian fundamentalists (Krichen 1995), Christian revivalists (born again Christians, Pentecostals) in Zimbabwe, Ghana, Nigeria and Zambia, and dissension among the Southern Sudanese, Touaregs, Ugandans, Joolas, and Zulus. It is necessary to reshape African administrations in a context in which they face technocrats, the private sector, and the informal strength of community organizations, and the abandonment of the heavy domination which they used to exert on African societies.

Where should we situate administrative power, how should we interpret the laws and relations governing political and economic interests and regulation? How should the different levels of power, responsibility and citizenship be organized? Given the fact that a long colonial and post-colonial tradition of administration (not governance) of the people and the economy has created instinctive suspicion and mistrust of administrators, can we reconcile African societies with the administration by separating the administrative function from the government?

Conclusion: An African Contribution to the Theory and Practice of Democratic Transition

In this introduction to a possible research programme, we have not sought to examine every element involved in the democratic transition process. Our main aim has been to open the debate, deliberately leaving aside certain themes which should be reintroduced, such as the issue of relations between the identity phenomenon and the multi-party system, the differential impacts of social groups, and of course the matter of external constraints, and the role of non-government organizations and civil society. This last issue is perhaps the most complex and the most controversial. And it is the matter of greatest concern to the donor organizations. It is clear that the perspective adopted which pits civil society against the state not only ignores the issue of the state, but also fails to consider the extraordinary work accomplished by social groups and communities which have had considerable impact on society from outside the state, without being for or against it.

Africa has instituted a new political phenomenon, the national conference, in a context of unprecedented political and economic crisis during the post-colonial period of its history. This new political instrument is unique to French-speaking Africa; our network plans to analyse this phenomenon by contrasting it with situations in English-speaking Africa and attempting to identify its roots (differences in management and colonial traditions). We hope to follow the programme outlined by Eboussi Boulaga (1993): gather a well-chosen, exhaustive body of speeches and papers presented at national conferences and create archives (diaries, life stories, etc.) of African democratic crises and develop research networks in order to organize and interpret the documentation and produce both primary documentation and secondary studies based on this material.

Along the same lines, such reflection should make it possible to register, in a wider and more complex context, the notion of political culture deficiency in Africa. This deficiency is said to be the cause of acclimatisation difficulties encountered by democracy in African countries while, one observes, specifically in advances favoured by political and economic liberalisation, a revival of old, political, social and ethnic divisions which are superimposed on new ones in countries like Cameroon, Côte d'Ivoire and Senegal, etc. There is thus an urgent need to take interest in these 'resurgences' by producing a chart of ethnic, regional and religious group allegiance and political voting since independence. In fact, in many cases, it seems that allegiances expressed during the nationalistic phase and repressed during the authoritarian phase are revived (redefined and transformed) in the new situation. This stability seems to confirm the existence of lines of force in political engagements in Africa.

The paragraph that concludes this reflection is not a conclusion *stricto sensu*. Rather, it is a classification which could help in understanding the establishment or restoration of open and multiform political systems, alternated by elections with challenges which are neither the exclusive and discriminatory control of resources (real or symbolic) by winners nor the demise or marginalisation of losers.

Trying to evaluate the significance of these moments, qualified as 'second independence' or 'democratic transition' by the most optimistic observers or as 'political liberalisation' by the most skeptical, is measuring the room for free speech, multiple, complex and competitive investments, combined with the production of regulatory mechanisms for arbitration and relations. In short, it means observing the ways in which political issues are dissociated from economic issues while trying to separate, definitively, the overlapping of the public and the private.

These abrupt and winding paths materialise through the establishment of mediation mechanisms and regulating institutions which finally endorse areas of jurisdiction for the exercise of State power and the plural expression of citizens' capacities; provided it is their aspiration, at least. Under these circumstances, should we accept to be abused by violence and the resulting regression it imposed on the democratic process — as was the case in Togo and Zaire. Or should we consent meekly to political manoeuvres such as redefinitions of the citizens' belonging to a community and electoral manipulations, as was the case in Zambia and Côte d'Ivoire, where manipulations have all resulted in maintaining authoritarian leadership in power?

The confrontation and muddling of arguments produced in the political and social spheres and the specialists' interpretation of such arguments, take us back to the problematics of the premises governing the qualification of a regime, political practices and citizen capacities. It is obvious that acts of elucidation are not limited only to an intellectual exercise. They also participate in the production of political systems.

Notes

1. The only exceptions were Botswana, Gambia, Mauritius, and Senegal after 1974, as these countries had more or less open political systems.

2. The media have popularized this explanation which offers external causes for the political upheaval in Africa. In retrospect, it seems increasingly evident that events in Eastern Europe only hid the changes underway in Africa and dulled their intensity. In the French-speaking world, frequent reference to the 'Discours de la Baule' (Speech at Baule) by President François Mitterand in 1990 as a founding event in the democratisation process in French Africa illustrates the externalist viewpoint quite clearly. This has been studied by J.-F. Bayart, in his article 'La Problématique de la démocratie en Afrique Noire, 'La Baule et puis après?' in *Politique africaine*, 43, October 1991 (5-20). Bayart refutes this interpretation and proves that while the speech at Baule was new in its form, it was nothing but a late response to demands for democracy. In conferences at the Governance Institute of CODESRIA in Dakar, in 1992, A. Bourgi interpretated Mitterand's speech as actually an attempt to control the democratic movement. See also Clough 1991; Hutchful 1995; Souley 1991.

3. These researchers, about a dozen in all, worked together under a Study Programme of the United Nations University, 'African Regional Perspectives' directed by Samir Amin and Peter Anyang' Nyong'o. As a point of departure for their research, they stressed the impact of the technocratic perspective on economic issues which tends to overshadow other political concerns, particularly the issue of democracy. Most of the results of the study programme can be found in Anyang' Nyong'o (1988).

4. The first document published by CODESRIA was used to form the working group: Mamdani *et al.* 1988. Following two workshops in Harare and Algiers, the group has just published: Mamdani and Wamba-dia-Wamba *African Studies in Social Movements and Democracy*, Dakar, CODESRIA, 1995. See also: M. Bratton and N. van der Walle, 'Towards Governance in Africa. Popular Demands and State Responses' in G. Hyden and M. Bratton (eds.), *Governance and Politics in Africa*, Boulder, Lynne Rienner, 1992, (27-56); R. Sandbrook, *The Politics of Africa's Economic Recovery*. Cambridge, Cambridge University Press, 1993, as well as the excellent article published in *Afrique Contemporaine*, 158, 2ème trimestre, 1991 (part 1), 3ème trimestre, 1991, (part 2).

5. I. Shivji, *South African Political Economy Monthly*, 3, (4), 1990 and 'The Pitfalls of the Debate on Democracy' in *Ifda Dossier*, 79, Oct./Dec. 1990, (55-58). In these articles, Shivji touched on one of the most interesting controversies among African researchers at CODESRIA. This debate was opened by P. Anyang' Nyong'o in an article published in *Africa Development*, XIII, 1, 1988, followed by contributions from Shivji, *op. cit.*; T. Mkandawire, CODESRIA Bulletin, 1, 1989 and 2, 1991; I. Mandaza and B.O. Gutto, *South African Political Economy Monthly*, 3, (4), 1990. Archie Mafeje presented a paper at CODESRIA's 7th General Assembly, 'Theory of Democracy and the African Discourse: Breaking Bread with my Fellow Travelers' which criticised the debate, soon to be published. Chole and Ibrahim 1995, in which P. Anyang' Nyong'o provided a temporary conclusion for the debate when he wrote:

> The political and economic case to be put for democracy can be advanced at two levels: one is the fact that almost all constitutions on which independent African states were established were democratic. Although practice rarely matches aspirations, the people still cherish the aspirations and struggle for them. No other agenda seems worth pursuing except that for which independence was fought. The struggle for democracy is still the centre of the agenda for the liberation of people.

6. In examining the democratic reform process, we will refer to the *Quality of Democracy Index* (QDI), according to which the first steps are the fall of the regime and the mobilization of the most vocal segments of society, *Africa Demos*, 2, 2, Feb. 1992.

7. This is the title of a book written by P. Anyang' Nyong'o, *op. cit.* The same imagery was used by J. Copans in *La longue marche de la modernité africaine: Savoirs, Intellectuels et Démocratie.* Paris, Karthala, 1990.

8. When we describe these countries as democratic, we are using the traditional criteria of multiple party systems, regular elections, freedom of the press, and freedom of assembly. Even among some of the authors who speak positively of these countries, there are reservations. J.D. Holm describes Botswana as a 'paternalistic democracy' in 'Rolling Back Autocracy in Africa: The Botswana case' in *Beyond Autocracy in Africa.* The Carter Center of Emory University, 1989; E. Sall and K. Sallah, 'Democratisation in the Gambia and the Current Debate on Democracy in Africa', 7th General Assembly of CODESRIA, Dakar, February 10-14, 1992; and C. Coulon consider Senegal a 'semi-democracy', 'Senegal: The Development and Fragility of a Semi-democracy' in L. Diamond *et al.* (eds.), *Democracy in Developing Countries.* Boulder, Lynne Rienner Publishers, 1988; and finally, M.C. Diop and M. Diouf on the 'incomplete democracy of Senegal', in *Le Sénégal sous Abdou Diouf.* Paris, Karthala, 1990.

9. R. Dahl, *Polyarchy: Participation and Opposition,* New Haven, Yale University Press, 1971. We should also cite another work by the same author, *Democracy and Its Critics,* New Haven, Yale University Press, 1989, in which he takes a diachronic perspective on the three successive transformations of the concept of democracy, from the Greek city-state (1) to the nation-state (2) to the present situation (3).

10. It is fundamental that we compare these different definitions of democracy with the theories put forward by C. Aké. In 'Rethinking African Democracy', *op. cit.*, Aké re-evaluates the classical arguments against democratic construction in Africa, in the present-day context. In another article, 'The Unique Case of African Democracy', in *International Affairs,* 69, (2), 1993, (239-244) he submits that democracy in Africa can only be built on the foundation of the singular realities of Africa, based on practical experience and spur of the moment creativity, and after hard struggle. This 'African democracy' which would ensure the participation of ordinary men and women would necessarily be different from the contemporary version of liberal democracy.

11. R. Lemarchand, 'Africa's Transitions to Democracy. An interim (and mostly pessimistic) Assessment' in *Africa Insight,* 22 (3), 1992 (178-185), p. 178. See also by the same author, 'Africa's Troubled Transitions' in *Journal of Democracy,* 3, (4), 1992, (98-109), in which he establishes a distinction between social movements capable of defeating a regime and the ability of certain social groups to create a new democratic power.

12. The choice of these regions is not haphazard, it reflects the combinations of elites and democracies studied in the existing literature. The authors of these studies use the role of the elite as an element of differentiation between 'stable democracies' and 'unstable democracies'. Among these works are: J. Highley and R. Gunther (eds.), *Elites and Democratic Consolidation in Latin America and Southern Europe.* Cambridge, Cambridge University Press, 1992; M.G. Burton and J. Highley, 'Elite Settlements' in *American Sociological Review,* 552, 1987 (295-307); T. R. Dye, *Who is Running America? The Reagan Years.* 3rd edit. Englewood Cliffs, N. J., Prentice Hall, 1983; R.D. Putnam, *The Comparative Study of Political Elites.* Englewood Cliffs, N. J., Prentice Hall, 176 and G. Moyser and M. Wagstaffe (eds.), *Research Methods for Elites Studies.* Boston, Allen and Unwin, 1987.

13. Indeed, in the Sahel, people known as 'arabisants' (The French term used to describe those educated in Arabic, in Arab countries) are not considered intellectuals.

14. J.-F. Bayart, *L'Etat en Afrique,* p. 179. The 'lines of historical continuity within the mechanisms of the state' (*Idem,* p. 181), which Bayart analysed in the Cameroon and other countries, have also been studied by other authors. In Senegal, D. Cruise O'Brien examined the 'success story' of the Muslim brotherhoods and the Senegalese state in *Saints and Politicians: Essays on the Organization of a Senegalese Peasant Society.* London, Cambridge University Press, 1975; and in 'Senegal' in J. Dunn (ed.), *West African States: Failure and Promise.* Cambridge, Cambridge University Press, 1978 (173-188); Sheldon Gellar, *Senegal: An African Nation between Islam and the West.* Boulder, Westview Press, 1982; in Brazzaville Congo, P.P. Rey, *Colonialisme, néocolonialisme et transition au capitalisme. Exemple de la Comilog au Congo-Brazzaville.* Paris, Maspéro, 1971. On the subject of Côte d'Ivoire, E. Terray wrote in fine literary style that:

> we can divide those who hold power into the *powers of the day* and the *powers of the night,* the powers dressed *in suits and ties* and the powers *wearing sarongs,* (...) If we must differentiate these groups, let us question our memories; the first system of government is associated with the discrete hum of the air conditioner; as for the second, we recall an evening when we had the privilege to be seated on the veranda of a very powerful individual, watching the workings of power in action. And so we can distinguish the *air-conditioned system* and the *veranda system.* (our italics), (*Afrique Plurielle, Afrique Actuelle. Hommage à Georges Balandier.* Paris, Karthala, 1986, (37-44), p. 42).

On Tanzania, D.-C. Martin wrote *Tanzanie. L'invention d'une culture politique.* Paris, Presses de la Fondation Nationale des Sciences Politiques/Karthala, 1988. On Kenya, G. Kitching, *Class and Economic Change in Kenya. The Making of an African Petite-Bourgeoisie.* New Haven, Yale University Press, 1980, and finally, on Africa in general, we can consult E. Terray (directing editor), *L'Etat contemporain en Afrique,* Paris, L'Harmattan, 1987.

15. Efforts have been made to adjust the theory, notably by: M. Bratton and N. van der Walle, *op. cit.* and 'Popular Protest and Political Transition in Africa', paper delivered at an International Conference on Civil Society in Africa sponsored by the Harry S. Truman Institute for International Peace at the Hebrew University, Jerusalem, Dec. 1992; Pearl Robinson, 'The National Conference in Francophone Africa' in *Comparative Studies in Society and History,* 26, (3), July 1994, (575-610) and 'Democratization: Understanding the Relationship Between Regime Change and the Culture of Politics' in *African Studies Review* 37, (1), 1994 (39-67), all of whom have worked extensively on these questions, and as well as by the main participants in the African Program of the Carter Center of Emory University which publishes the newsletter *Africa Demos.* However, all these works have solid theoretical ties to the following studies: L. Diamond, J.J. Linz and S.M. Lipset (eds.), *Democracy in Developing Countries: Africa,* Vol. 2, 1988, *Asia,* Vol. 3 and *Latin America,* Vol. 4, 1989, Boulder, Lynne Rienner Publishers; G.A. O'Donnell, P. Schmitter, (eds.), *Transitions from Authoritarian Rule,* 4 vol., Baltimore, Johns Hopkins University Press, 1986; S. Huntington, *op. cit.;* R.D. Putnam, R. Leonardi and R. Nanetti, *Making Democracy Work: Civic traditions in Modern Italy.* Princeton, Princeton University Press, 1993; and A. Przeworski, *Democracy and the Market: Political and Economic Reforms in Eastern Europe and Latin America.* Cambridge, Cambridge University Press, 1991.

16. This instrument for measuring democracy was established by the *Africa Governance Program* of the *Carter Center of Emory University,* Atlanta, USA. The QDI has been published in *Africa Demos,* Vol. II, Feb. 1992.

17. For a similar analysis, see also J.-F. Bayart, who writes in his Preface to *La Politique par le bas...*, *op. cit.* that the struggle for multiple party systems is often a transformation of internal struggles between factions in established regimes, p. 17.

18. In his contribution to the volume edited by M. Mamdani and Wamba-dia-Wamba, Z. Krichen, 'The Islamist Fundamentalist Movement in Tunisia 1970-1990: History and Language', *op. cit.* (544-601), questions whether the fundamentalist movement is part of civil society. In his text and that of his compatriot, A. Zghal, 'The Bread Riots and the Crisis of the One-Party System in Tunisia' in M. Mamdani and Wamba-dia-Wamba (eds.), *op. cit.* (99-132), we can discover respectively a 'chronology of events (591-598)' and an 'appendix sequence of the bread riots (130-132)'.

19. For example, among the published studies to which we have had access, such as the volume edited by M. Mamdani and Wamba-dia-Wamba, except for the two texts cited above, all the other analyses concentrated on identifying the nature of the impact of social movements on struggles to enlarge the democratic arena rather than on the phases of transition. However, among the unpublished studies undertaken by CODESRIA's Multinational Working Group on Legal Succession and Political Transitions in Africa, a study by J. Gandaho and S. Varissou, 'Le Renouveau Démocratique au Bénin ou la Révolution négociée' applies the categories set out in *Africa Demos* almost directly. Two studies coordinated by B. Barry, one on Mali and one on the Cameroon, follow each day of the riots that opened the way to the fall of the authoritarian regime in Mali and in the Cameroon, the transition to a multiple party system while maintaining a repressive system and contested elections.

20. Abubakar Momoh wrote on the subject of 'area boys': 'The area boys as a social category became preponderant, popularised and organised from about 1986 when the Structural Adjustment Programme took its full course. Hence today, any form of crime or criminal in the entire South-Western Nigeria is identifiable or traceable to the area boys. The area boys are the equivalent of 'Yandaba' in Hausaland, they are also called *alaayes, Omo oni ile* (son of the soil or landlords), *sweet urchins, government pickin, untouchables,* or *alright sir*. 'The South-Western Nigeria Case Study', Paper presented at the West African Long Term Perspective Study (WALTPS), ADB-CINERGIE Conference, October 11-13, Lagos, 1993, p. 28.

References

Adam, H., 1993, 'Frantz Fanon as a Democratic Theorist' in *African Affairs : The Journal of the Royal African Society*, 92 (369).

Ake, C., 1991, 'Rethinking Democracy', *Journal of Democracy*, 2, (Winter), 32-44.

Ake, C., 1993, 'The Unique Case of African Democracy', in *African Affairs*, 69 (2), Africa and Democracy, April, (239-244).

Amin, Samir, 1993, *Itinéraire Intellectuel*, Paris, L'Harmattan, 1993.

Anyang' Nyong'o, P., 1987, *Popular Struggles for Democracy in Africa*, London, Zed Press (édition anglaise).

Anyang' Nyong'o, P., 1988 (eds.), Afrique. La longue marche vers la démocratie. Etat autoritaire est résistances populaires, Paris, Publisud, Ftm, UNU.

Anyang' Nyong'o, P., 1995, 'Discourses on Democracy in Africa', in E. Chole & J. Ibrahim (eds.) 1995, *Democratisation Processes in Africa*, Dakar, CODESRIA, 29-42.

Bakary, Tessy, 'Transition politique et succession en Côte d'Ivoire', in M. C. Diop et M. Diouf, *Des pouvoirs mérités aux pouvoirs élus. Les nouvelles figures du politiques en Afrique* (A paraître 1998).

Bayart, J. F.; Mbembe, A.; Toulabor, C., 1992, *La politique par le bas en Afrique noire. Contributions à une problématique de la démocratie,* Paris, Karthala.

Blanquart, P., 1992, 'L'avenir d'une Déliaison' in *Autrement,* 127, février, (92-104).

Bratton, M. et N. Van der Walle, 1992, 'Popular Protest and Political Transition in Africa' in *Comparative Politics,* 24, (4), (419-442).

Bratton, M., 1992, 'Civil Society and Political Transition in Africa', Paper delivered at an International Conference on Civil Society in Africa sponsored by the Harry S. Truman Institute for International Peace at the Hebrew University, Jerusalem, December.

Coulon, C., 1988, 'Sénégal : The Development and Fragility of a Semi-democracy' in L. Diamond *et al.* (eds.), Democracy in Developing Countries, Boulder, Lynne Rienner Publishers.

Diamond, L., J. J. Linz & S. M. Lipset, 1989 (eds), *Democracy in Developping Countries : Africa,* Vol. 2, *Asia,* Vol. 3 et *Latin America,* Vol. 4, 1989, Boulder, Lynne Rienner Publishers.

Diarrah, C. O., 1993, 'Les ambiguïtés et les difficultés de la concrétisation opérationnelle du projet démocratique du Mali', Communication présentée à l'atelier sur les Villes ouest-africaines, Etude des perspectives à long terme de l'Afrique de l'Ouest, OCDE/BAD, Dakar, 15-17 novembre.

Diop, M. C. et M. Diouf, 1996, (sous la direction), Successions Légales et Transitions Démocratiques. A paraître, CODESRIA.

Diop, M.C. et Diouf, M., 1990, *Le Sénégal sous Abdou Diouf,* Paris, Karthala.

Eboussi Boulaga, F., 1993, Les Conférences Nationales en Afrique Noire. Une Affaire à suivre, Paris, Khartala.

El Kenz, A., 1989 (ed), *L'Algérie et la Modernité,* Dakar, CODESRIA.

El Kenz, A., 1995, 'De l'espérance du développement à la violence identitaire : Rapport algérien' in *Bulletin du CODESRIA,* 2, (2-8).

Geshiere, P., 1995, *Sorcellerie et politique, La viande des autres,* Paris, Karthala.

Krichen, Z., 1995, 'The Islamic Fundamentalist Movement in Tunisia, 1970-90', in Mamdani et Wamba-dia-Wamba (eds.), (544-601).

Mafeje, A., 'Theory of Democracy and the African Discourse: Breaking Bread with my Fellow-travellers', in E. Chole & J. Ibrahim (eds.) 1995, *Democratisation Processes in Africa, Problems and Prospects,* Dakar, CODESRIA, pp.5-28.

Mamdani, M. et Wamba-dia-Wamba, 1995 (eds), *Social Movements in Africa,* Dakar, CODESRIA.

Mamdani, M., 1995, 'Contradictory Class Perspectives on the Question of Democracy : The Case of Uganda' in P. Anyang' Nyong'o (1988) et son introduction à M. Mamdani & E. Wamba-dia-Wamba (eds.), *African Perspectives on Social Movement and Democracy* Dakar, CODESRIA.

Martin, G., 1993, 'Preface: Democratic Transitions in Africa', in Issue: A Quarterly Journal of Opinion, 21 (1-2).

Mbembe, Achille, 1992, 'Traditions de l'autoritarisme et problèmes de gouvernement en Afrique subsaharienne', *Afrique et Développement,* 17 (1), (37-64).

Mbembe, A., 1994, 'Déflation de l'Etat. Civilité et citoyenneté en Afrique noire' in Gemdev (ed), *L'intégration régionale dans le monde. Innovations et ruptures* Paris, Karthala, (273-286), p.277.

Mkandawire, Thandika, 1991, *Gouvernance démocratique en Afrique : Un projet du CODESRIA*, Dakar.

Momoh, Abubakar, 1993, 'The South-Western Nigeria Case Study', Paper presented at the West African Long Term Perspective Study (WALTPS), ADB-CINERGIE Conference, 11-13 October Lagos, p.28.

O'Donnell, Guillermo and Schmitter, Philippe C.,1986, *Transitions from Authoritarian Rule: Tentative Conclusions, About Uncertain Democracies,* London, John Hopkins University Press, XII-81p.

Oyugi Walter, O. *et al.*, 1988 (eds.), *Democratic Theory and Practice in Africa* London, James Currey.

Przeworski, A., 1991, *Democracy and the Market : Political and Economic Reforms in Eastern Europe and Latin America* Cambridge, Cambridge University Press.

Putman, R. D., R Leonardi et R. Nanetti, 1983, *Making Democracy Work : Civic Traditions in Modern Italy.* Princeton, Princeton Universty Press.

Richards, P., 1993, 'Liberia and Sierra Leone' (draft), forthcoming, in O. W. Furley (ed.), Conflict in Africa.

Robinson, Pearl, 1994a, 'The National Conference in Francophone Africa' in *Comparative Studies in Society and History,* 26, (3); July.

Robinson, Pearl, 1994b, 'Democratization : Understanding the Relationship Between Regime Change and The Culture of Politics' in *African Studies Review* 37, (1).

Sall, E. et K. Sallah, 1992, 'Democratisation in the Gambia and the Current Debate on Democracy in Africa'. 7ème Assemblée générale du CODESRIA, Dakar, 10-14 February.

Sandbrook, R. 1988, 'Liberal Democracy in Africa : A Socialist-Revisionist Perspective' in Revue canadienne d'études africaines, 22, (2), (240-267), Table 1.

Schlegel, J. L., 1992, 'Entre Religion et Démocratie : Concorde et Conflits' in *Autrement*, 127, février, (167-177).

Sindjoun, L., 1998, 'Le Président de la République à l'épreuve du changement politique au Cameroun: de l'alternance néo-patrimoniale à la "Transition démocratique"', M. C. Diop et M. Diouf, *Des pouvoirs hérités aux pouvoirs élus. Les nouvelles figures du politique en Afrique* (A paraître, CODESRIA, 1998).

Zghal, Z., 1995, 'The Bread Riots and the Crisis of the One-Party System in Tunisia' in M. Mamdani et Wamba-dia-Wamba (eds.) (99-132).

Bibliography

This bibliography comprises references in English and French. It is divided into six (6) parts namely:

- the first section is general;

- the second section collates CODESRIA publications on the subject;

- the third and most substantial section lists out documents on Africa;

- a fourth section on Latin America;

- a fifth section on Asia;

- and a sixth section on Eastern Europe.

The interest from having work on other regions in this bibliography is that it provides us with documentation that could allow a comparative study between democratic transition in Africa and in other continents.

The identification of references in each part is facilitated by an alphabetical sub-classification.

Finally, the references preceded by an asterisk could be found at the CODESRIA Documentation and Information Centre (CODICE).

Section 1: General

* Beetham, David, 1994, 'Conditions for Democratic Consolidation' *Review of African Political Economy*, Vol. 21, No. 60, June, (157-172).

Dahl, R., 1971, *Polyarchy: Participation and Opposition*, New Haven, Yale University Press.

Dahl, R., 1989, *Democracy and Its Critics*, New Haven, Yale University Press.

* Di Palma, Giuseppe, 1990, *To Craft Democracies: An Essay on Democratic Transitions*, Berkeley, University of California Press, 248p.

Greenberg, Douglas, (ed.), 1993, *Constitutionalism and Democracy: Transitions in the Contemporary World*, 416 p.

Haggard, Stephen, 1995, *The Political Economy of Democratic Transitions*, Princeton University Press.

Section 2: CODESRIA

* 'Africa in the 1980's: State and Social Science', *Africa Development*, Special Issue, 15 (3-4).

* Ahipeaud, Joseph Martial, 1992, 'Les étudiants et les élèves dans la transition politique ivoirienne', Dakar, CODESRIA, 11-14 mai, 23p, *Conférence sur Démocratie et droits de l'homme en Afrique: Facteurs internes et externes*, Harare Zimbabwe.

* Akindes, Francis,1996, *Les mirages de la démocratie en Afrique subsaharienne francophone*, Dakar, CODESRIA, 246p.

* Amin, Samir, 1989, 'La question démocratique dans le tiers monde contemporain',*Africa Development*, Dakar, CODESRIA, 14 (2), (5-26).

* Amuwo, Kunle, 1993, 'Transition Planning in Nigeria: A Critique of the Military-Civil Transiting Variant', *Africa Development*, Vol. XVIII, No. 1, (87-98).

* Campbell, H., 1993, 'Angolan Woman and the Electoral Process in Angola',*Africa Development*, 18 (2), (23-63).

* Chege, M., 1993, 'The Kenya December 1992 General Elections: Opposition Leaders Play into the Hands of the Ruling Kanu Party', *CODESRIA Bulletin*, 1.

* Diouf, M., 1993, 'Senegal's February 1993 Elections: New Factors in the Political Arena', *CODESRIA Bulletin*, 2.

* El-Tigane Mahmoud, Mahgoun, 1992, 'African Transition to Democracy: The Case of Sudan', Dakar, CODESRIA, *Conference on Democracy and Human Rights in* Africa, Harare Zimbabwe, 11-14 May, 27p.

* Hutchful, Eboe, 1993, 'Military Issues in the Democratic Transitions in Africa', Dakar, CODESRIA, Accra, Ghana, 21-23 April, 14p.

* Ibrahim, Jibrin, 1992, 'Democratic Transitions in Africa: Successes and Failures on the Expansion of Democratic Space', Dakar, CODESRIA, *Conference on Democracy and Human Rights in Africa*, Harare, Zimbabwe, 11-14 May 31p.

* Ibrahim, Jibrin, 1993, 'Democratic Political Succession in Niger Republic: The 1993 Elections', *CODESRIA Bulletin*, 2.

* Ibrahim, Jibrin, 1993, 'History as Iconolast: Left Stardom and the Debate on Democracy', *CODESRIA Bulletin*, 1.

* Ibrahim, Jibrin and Chole, Eshetu, (eds.), 1995, *Democratisation Processes in Africa: Problems and Prospects,* Paris, CODESRIA, 147p.

* Mafeje, A., 1993, 'An Icon and African Perspectives on Democracy. A Commentary on Jibrin Ibrahim's Views', *CODESRIA Bulletin,* 2.

* Mama, Amina, 1995, 'Feminism or Femocracy? State Feminism and Democratization in Nigeria', *Africa Development,* 20 (1), (37-58).

* Naidoo, G., (eds.), 1991, *Reform and Revolution: South Africa in the Nineties,* Dakar, Johannesburg, CODESRIA Book Series, Skotaville Publications, 227 p.

* Ninsin, Kwame, A., 1992, 'Democratic Transitions: Successes and Failures', Dakar, CODESRIA, *Conference on Democracy and Human Rights in Africa,* Harare, Zimbabwe, 11-14 May, 11p.

* Ninsin, Kwame, A., 1993, 'Some Problems in Ghana's Transition to Democratic Governance', *Africa Development,* Vol XVIII, No. 2, (5-22).

* Onana, Renner-Mamert-Lie, 1993, 'La problématique de la transition démocratique en Afrique post-coloniale', Yaoundé, Université de Yaoundé II, thèse de doctorat de 3e cycle, Relations internationales, Université de Yaoundé II, Institut des relations internationales du Cameroun, xi-742p.

* Ossebi, Henri, 1992, 'Production démocratique et transition post-totalitaire au Congo: portée et limites d'une expérience', *7ème Assemblée générale, conférence sur le processus de démocratisation en Afrique: problèmes et perspectives,* Dakar, CODESRIA, 10-14 février, 21p.

* Sindjoun, L., 1994, 'La cour suprême, la compétition électorale et la continuité politique au Cameroun: la construction de la démocratisation passive', *Africa Development,* 19 (2), (21-69).

* Vieira, Juscelino Emanuel, 1992, 'Democraci e es Direitos Humanos em Cabo Verde: Limites de Experiencias', Dakar, CODESRIA, 1992, *Conférence sur démocratie et droits de l'homme en Afrique: Facteurs internes et externes,* Harare, Zimbabwe, 11-14 mai, 10p.

* Wodie, Francis, 1992, 'Problématique de la transition démocratique en Afrique', *7ème Assemblée générale, Conference sur le Processus de démocratisation en Afrique: problèmes et perspectives,* Dakar, Sénégal, 10-14 février, 15p.

Section 3: Africa

Abba, S. M., 1994, 'Les problèmes de la presse indépendante au Niger', *Politique Africaine,* 54, juin.

* Abbink, J., 1995, 'Ethnicité et démocratisation: le dilemme éthiopien', *Politique Africaine,* 57, mars (135-141).

* Adam, H. and Moodley, K., 1993, 'South Africa: the Opening of the Apartheid Mind', in McGarry J. et Oleary B. (eds.), *The Politics of Ethnic Regulation,* London and New York, Routledge, (226-250)'.

* Adam, H., 1994, 'Formation and Recognition of New States: Somaliland in Constrat to Eritrea', *Review of African Political Economy,* 21 (59), March, (21-38).

Adamon, Afize D., 1994, *Le renouveau démocratique au Bénin: la Conférence nationale des forces vives et la période de transition,* Paris, (ed.), l'Harmattan, 223p.

Adedeji A., 1994, 'An Alternance for Africa', *Journal of Democracy,* 5 (4), October, (119-132).

* *African Development Review,* 1991, 'Democracy, Recovery and Development in Africa', *African Development Review,* Special, 3 (2), December, (179-195).

* *Afrique 2000,* 1993, *La démocratisation en Afrique, Afrique 2000,* numéro spécial, 14, juillet-décembre, (39-82).

* *Afrique contemporaine,* 1994, 'Togo: la constitution de la IVème République', *Afrique Contemporaine,* 170, 2ème trimestre, (54-74).

Agbese, P. O. and Kieh, G. K, 1992, 'Military Disengagement from African Politics: The Nigerian Experience', *Africa Spectrum,* 1, (5-23).

Agbese, P. O. and Kieh, G .K., 1992, 'Nigeria: Transition to Democracy and the Pathological Elite Thesis', *Zeitschrift für Afrikastudien,* 15-16,.

Agbobli, A. K., 1991, 'Prolégomènes de la Conférence nationale du Togo',*Afrique 2000,* 7, novembre, (55-73).

Agboyibo, Y., 1991, 'Les Droits de l'homme au Togo',*Etudes,* 374 (5), mai, (609-613).

Ahmed, D. A. and Dehli, A., 1993, 'La longue lutte des Afars',*Politique internationale,* 61, Autumn, (163-185).

* Aicardi de Saint-Paul, M., 1992, 'Présentation de la constitution du Burkina Faso', *Afrique Contemporaine,* 159, 3ème trimestre, (74-77).

* Aicardi de Saint-Paul, M., 1992, 'Afrique du Sud: le référendum du 17 mars 1992', *Afrique Contemporaine,* 164, 4ème trimestre, (26-30).

* Aicardi de Saint-Paul, M., 1994, 'Afrique du Sud: un homme une voix',*Afrique Contemporaine,* 171, juillet-septembre, (3-16).

* Ake, C., 1992, 'Devaluing Democracy',*Journal of Democracy,* 3 (3), juillet, (37-44).

Ake, C., 1993b, 'What is the Problem of Ethnicity in Africa?',*Transformation,* 22.

Akinboye, S. O., 1991, 'Apartheid and Democratization Process in South Africa',*Review of African Political Affairs,* 5 (1-2), July-December.

Akindele, S. T. and Ajula, C. O., 1992, 'Democratic Transition in Africa, A Psychological Perspective', in Caron B., Gboyega A. and Osaghae E. (eds), *Democratic Transition in Africa,* Ibadan, CREDU, Proceedings of a Symposium, 436 p., (83-100).

Akwetey, E. O., 1994, *Trade Unions and Democratization: a Comparative Study of Zambia and Ghana* Stockholm, University of Stockholm, 128 p.

* Alden, C. and Simpson, M., 1993, 'Mozambique: A Delicate Peace',*Journal of Modern African Studies,* 31 (1), pp. 109-130.

Allen, C., (ed.) ,1993, *Africa Bibliography: 1992 (Works on Africa Publishing During 1992),* Edinburgh University Press, 480 p.

* Allen, C., Baylies, C. and Szeftel, M., 1992, 'Surviving democracy?',*Review of African Political Economy,* 54, juillet, (3-10).

Allison, L., 1994, 'On the Gap Between Theories of Democracy and Theories of Democratization?', *Democratizarion,* 1 (1), Spring, (8-26).

Amadife, E., 1992, 'The Challenge of Democratization in Nigeria: Involvement or Alienation of the Military?', *Ufahamu,* 20 (1),Winter, (30-43).

Amin, Samir, 1993, *Itinéraire intellectuel,* Paris, L'Harmattan.

Amundsen, I., 1993, 'Afropessimism: Response from Below?' in Oftsad, A. and Wiig, A. (eds.), *Development Theory: Recent Trends,* Bergen, Chr. Michelsen Institute, Proceedings of the NFU Annual Conference 1992, Report 6, 285p., (135-154).

45

Amuwo, K., 1992a, 'The International (and Domestic) Context of Democratic Transition in Africa. Roadblocks to Democracy', in Caron B., Gboyega A. et Osaghae E. (eds.), *Democratic Transition in Africa*, Ibadan, CREDU, Proceedings of a Symposium, 436.p.,(3-27).

* Amuwo, K., 1992b, 'Treetop Politics vs Grassroots Democracy in Nigeria: Some Theoretical and Methodological Queries', *Africa*, 47 (4), (617-626).

Andreassen, B.A., Geisler, G. and Tostensen, A., 1992, *Setting a Standard for Africa? Lessons from the 1991 Zambian Elections*, Bergen, Chr. Michelsen Institute, Report 5, 137 p.

Andrew, E., 'La Conférence nationale est-elle la solution?', *Parlements et Francophonie*, 85, avril-juin 1992, (47-53).

* Anstee, M.J., 1995, 'L'ONU et le maintien de la paix', *Politique africaine*, 57, mars, (103-111).

* Anstey, M., 1992, 'Mediation in the South African Transition: A Critical Review of Developments, Problems and Potentials', *Genève-Afrique*, 30 (2), (141-163).

* Anyang' Nyong'o, P., 1992a, 'Democratization Process in Africa', *Review of African Political Economy*, 54, juillet, (97-105).

* Anyang' Nyong'o, P., 1992b, 'Africa: The Failure of the One Party Rule', *Journal of Democracy*, 3(1), (90-96).

Apter, D. and Rosberg, C.G. (eds.), 1994, *Political Development and the New Realism in the New Sub-Saharan Africa*, Charlottesville and London, University Press of Virginia, 339p.

Ariffin, Y., 1992, 'Développement et démocratie:ajustement macroéconomique et transformations micropolitiques', *Trimestre du Monde*, 17, 1er trimestre, (61-89).

Assemblée internationales des parlementaires de langue française, 1993, *Le développement institutionnel: l'Etat de droit pluraliste, action conjointe de la puissance publique et de la société civile*, Paris, AIPLF-PARDOC, Ibiscus, 126 p.

Assoumou, Ndoutoume D., 1993, *Du Mvett: l'orage, processus de démocratisation conté par un diseur de Mvett*, Paris, l'Harmattan, 219p.

Austin, D., 1993, 'Reflexion on African Politics: Prospero, Ariel and Caliban', *African Affairs*, 69 (2), Africa and Democracy, aApril, (203-222).

Ayee, J. R. A., 1992, 'Decentralization Under Ghana's Fourth Republican Constitution', *Verfassung und Recht in Ubersee*, 25, (394-406).

Ayeni, V., 1993, 'The Executive Presidency as Concomitant of Multipartyism in Africa: An Assessment', *Indian Journal of Political Science*, 54 (2), April-June, (161-193).

Ayittey, G., 1993, *Africa Betrayed*, Macmillan Press, 368 p.

Ayoade, J. A. A. *et al.* (eds.), 1992, *Women and Politics in Nigeria*, Malthouse Press.

Baechler, J., 1992, 'Des institutions démocratiques pour l'Afrique', *Revue juridique et politique, indépendance et coopération*, 2, avril-juin, (163-181).

Bagachwa, M. S. D. and Mbelle, A. Y. V. (eds.), 1993, *Economic Policy under a Multiparty System in Tanzania*, Dar-es-Salaam, Dar-es-Salaam University Press.

Bakary T., 1990, 'De la démocratie à l'ivoirienne à la démocratie ivoirienne', *Géopolitique Africaine*, 13 (2), mai, (45-62).

Bakary, T., 1990, 'Mutations au Nord, interrogations au Sud', *Etudes internationales*, 21 (3), septembre, (469-485).

Bakary, T., 1992a, *La démocratie par le haut en Côte d'Ivoire*, Paris, L'Harmattan.

Bakary, T., 1992b, 'Pour une approche non partisane de la démocratie en Afrique',*Afrique 2000*, 9 mai, (27-35).

Bakary, T., 1992c, 'Des militaires aux avocats: une autre forme de coup d'Etat, la Conférence Nationale souveraine', *Géopolitique africaine*, 15 (2), septembre-octobre, (7).

Bakary, T., 1991, 'Au Bénin les premiers pas d'un groupe panafricain d'observation', *Géopolitique africaine*, 14 (4), septembre, (53-60).

* Balima, S. A., 1992, 'Réflexions sur l'Afrique et la démocratie', *Afrique 2000*, 11, novembre, (49-54).

* Baloro, J., 1992, 'The Human Right to Free Association and Assembly and Multi-party Democracy: A Study of the Law and Practice in Swaziland', *Africa Insight*, 22 (3), (206-211).

Balta, P., 1992, 'La Mauritanie à l'heure du multipartisme', *Confluence en Méditerranée*, 3, Spring, (130-136).

Banegas, R., 1993, 'Les transitions démocratiques mobilisation collective et fluidité politique', *Cultures et conflits*, 12, Winter, (105-140).

* Banga-Bane, J., 1992, 'Pourquoi la violence? Réflexions sur les moments douloureux de la transition démocratique au Zaïre', *Zaïre-Afrique*, 263, mars, (133-141).

* Bangoura, D., 1993, 'Armées et défis démocratiques en Afrique',*Afrique 2000*, 12 janvier-mars, (111-122).

Bangura, Y., 1992, 'Authoritarian Rule and Democracy in Africa', *in* Rudebeck L. (ed.), *When Democracy Makes sense: Studies in the Democratic Potential of Third World Popular Mouvements*, Stockholm, AKUT, 399 p., (60-104).

* Banock, M., 1993, *Le Processus de démocratisation en Afrique le cas camerounais*, Paris, l'Harmattan, 252 p.

Barber, J., 1994, 'South Africa: the Search for Identity', *International Affairs Bulletin*, 70 (1), (67-82).

Barbier, J. C., 1994, 'Afrique du Sud: vers la démocratie', *Esprit*, 7, (40-65).

Baregu, M., 1993, 'The Economic Origins of Political Liberalization and Future Prospects', *in* Bagachwa M.S.D. et Mbelle A.V.Y. (eds.), *Economy Policy under a Multiparty System in Tanzania*, Dar-es-Salaam, Dar-es-Salaam University Press, (105-123).

* Barkan, J. D., 1993, 'Kenya: Lessons from a Flawed Election', *Journal of Democracy*, 4(3), July.

* Barsh, R. L., 1992, 'Democratization and Development', *Human Rights Quaterly*, 14 (1) February, (120-134).

* Barya, J., 1993, 'The New Political Conditionalities of Aid: An Independent View From Africa', *IDS Bulletin*, 24 (1), January.

* Bauzon, K. E., (ed.), 1992, *Development and Democratization in the Third World: Myths, Homes and Realities*, Washington, Crane Russak, 344p.

* Bayart, J. F., 1993a, La politique de la France de Charybde en Scylla? *Politique africaine*, 49, mars.

Bayart, J. F., 1993b, 'Fin de partie au Sud du Sahara', in Michailof S. (ed), *La France et l'Afrique: Vade-mecum pour un nouveau voyage*, Paris, Karthala, 510p., (112-129).

* Baynham, S., 1993, 'Will Africa's Democracy survive?', *Africa Insight*, 23 (4); (182-183).

Beattyn, D., 1992, 'The Rule (and Role) of Law in the New South Africa: Some Lessons from Abroad', *South African Law Journal,* 109 (3), (408-427).

* Beckman, B., 1993, 'The Liberation of Civil Society: Neo Liberal Ideology and Political Theory', *Review of African Political Economy,* 58, November, (20-33).

* Beetham, D. et al., (eds.), 1994, *Defining and Measuring Democracy,* London, Sage, Sage Modern Politics Series: 36, VIII+228p.

* Bekker, J. C., 1993, 'The Role of Chiefs in a Future South African Constitutional Dispensation', *Africa Insight,* 23 (4), (200-204).

Bellamy, W. C., 1993, 'La formation d'une identité sud africaine: l'engagement des personnes classées white dans le mouvement démocratique', Université Paris I, Thèse, de sociologie, sciences sociales, 376 p.

* Benoist, J. R., 1992, 'Les clercs et la démocratie', *Afrique contemporaine,* 164, octobre-décembre, (178-193).

Berat, L. and Shain, Y., 1992, 'Provisional Governments in Democratization. The International Interim Government. Model and the Case of Namibia', *Co-Existence,* 29 (3), September, (19-40).

Bergen, Chr. Michelsen Institute, Proceedings of the NFU Annual Conference 1992, Report 6, 285 p., (106-118).

* Berrubé, C., 1993, 'Entre démocratisation et agitation sociale: le Mali, un pays qui se cherche', *Afrique 2000,* 20 janvier-février-mars, (95-106).

* Bertrand, J., 'Une émeute sur la côte kényane', *Afrique contemporaine,* 170, 1994, (20-36).

* Bertrand, M., 1992, 'Un an de transition politique: de la révolte à la troisième République', *Politique africaine,* 47, octobre, (9-22).

* Bhagwati, J., 1992, 'Democracy and Development', *Journal of Democracy,* 3 (3), July, (37-44).

Biagiotti, I., 1995, 'Coopération: Afrique, droits de l'homme, démocratie et conditionnalité. Eléments des discours allemands', *L'Afrique politique.*

Bienen, H. and Herbst, J., 1991, 'Authoritarianism and Democracy in Africa', *in* Rustow D. A. et Erickson K. P. (eds.), *Comparative Political Dynamics,* New York, Harper Collins, (211-232).

* Bigo, D., 1993, 'La délégitimation des pouvoirs entre politique du ventre et démocratie', *in* Conac G. (ed.), *L'Afrique en Transition vers le pluralisme politique,* Paris, Economica, 517p., (155-163).

* Bizeck, J. P., 1991, 'Zambia: the Myth and Realities of one Participatory Democracy', *Genève-Afrique,* 29 (2), (9-24).

* Blackwell, 1992, 'L'évolution politique du Malawi', *Afrique contemporaine,* 164, 4ème trimestre, (17-25).

Blancq, B., 1994, 'Congo: Corruption et résistance au changement', *L'Afrique politique, Vue sur la démocratisation à marée basse,* (191-198).

Blaney, D. L. and Pasha, M. K., 1993, 'Civil Society and Democracy in the Third World: Ambiguities and Historical Possibilities', *Studies in Comparative International Development,* 28 (1), 1993, (3-24).

Bluwey, G. K., 1992, 'Democracy at Bay: The Frustrations of African Liberals', *in* Caron B., Gboyega A. and Osaghae E. (eds.), *Democratic Transition in Africa,* Ibadan, CREDU, Proceedings of a Symposium, 436 p., (39-49).

48

Boilley P., 1994, 'La démocratisation au Mali: un processus exemplaire', Relations internationales et stratégiques, 14, Summer, (119-121).

Boillot, F., 1992-93, 'L'église catholique face aux processus de changements politiques du début des années 1990', Année africaine, (115-144).

Bonenge, J. R., 1995, 'Une lecture de la démocratie au travers de Zaïre-Afrique de 1994', Zaïre-Afrique, 30 (291), janvier.

Bosch, A., 1994, 'Les premières élections générales en Afrique du Sud', Politique africaine, 54, juin, (127-143).

Bouchard, J. C., 1992, La longue marse de la démocratie gabonaise, Libreville, Gadedip, 159 p.

Boumankani, B., 1990, 'L'évolution récente de la démocratie au Congo', Alternative démocratique dans le tiers monde, 2, juillet-décembre, (177-185).

Bourgi, A., 1990, 'L'Afrique: le réveil de la démocratie', Afrique 2000, 1, avril, (63-67).

* Bourmaud, D. and Quantin, P., 1991, 'Les chemins de la démocratie', Politique africaine, 43, Special Issue, p. 187.

* Bourmaud, D., 1992, 'Kenya: Démocratie et indépendance', Politique africaine, 47, octobre, (135-140).

* Bourmaud, D., 1993, 'Les élections au Kenya: victoire ou répit?', Politique africaine, 49, mars, (141-145).

Bouvier, P., 1992, 'L'Afrique politique face à son devenir', Civilisations, 50 (2), (232-252).

Bratton, Michael, 1992, 'Zambia Starts Over', Journal of Democracy, Vol. 3, No.2, April (81-84).

Bratton, M. and Rothchild, D., 1992, 'The Institutional Bases of Governance in Africa', in Hyden G. and Bratton M. (eds.), Governance and Politics in Africa, Boulder, Lynne Rienner Publishers, 329 p., (263-284).

* Bratton, M. and van der Walle, N., 1994, 'Neopatrimonial Regime and Political Transition in Africa', World Politics, 46 (4).

Bratton, M. and Liatto-Katundu, B., 1994, 'A Focal Group Assessment of Political Attitudes in Zambia', African Affairs, 93 (373), octobre, (535-563).

* Breitinger, E., 1993, 'Lamentations Patriotics Writers, Censors and Politics in Cameroon', African Affairs, 92 (369), (557-575).

Breton, J. M., 1991, 'La transition vers la démocratie au Congo', Revue congolaise de droit, 10, juillet-décembre 1991, (13-40).

Brett, E. A., 1994, 'Rebuilding Organization Capacity in Uganda under the National Resistance Movement', Journal of Modern African Studies, 32 (1), March 1994.

Brogden, M, and Shearing, C. D., 1993, Policing for a New South Africa, London, Routledge, 256 p.

* Broomh, N. K., 1993, 'Pouvoir politique, territoires polyethniques et renouveau démocratique en Afrique', Afrique 2000, 20, janvier-février-mars, (29-34).

Brutus, D., 1993, 'Literature and Change in South Africa', Research in African Literatures, 24 (3), (101-104).

Brynen Rex, Korany Bahgat, Noble Paul, (eds.), 1995, Political Liberalization and Democratization in the Arab World: Theoretical Perspectives Vol. 1, Boulder, Lynne Rienner Publishers, Inc., x-350p.

* Buijtenhuijs, R. 1993, *La conférence nationale souveraine du Tchad: un essai d'histoire immédiate*, Paris, Karthala, 212p.

Buijtenhuijis, R., 1994a, 'Tchad: Une conférence nationale et des massacres', *L'Afrique politique, Vue sur la Démocratisation à marée basse*, (17-24).

Buijtenhuijs, R., 1994b, 'Les partis politiques africaines ont-ils des projets de sociétés? L'exemple du Tchad', *Politique africaine*, 56, décembre (119-136).

* Buijtenhuijs, Rob and Thiriot, Céline, 1995, *Démocratisation en Afrique au Sud du Sahara 1992-1995: un bilan de la littérature*, Bordeaux, Centre d'étude d'Afrique noire, 217p.

* Bullier, A. J., 1994, 'La constitution intérimaire d'Afrique du Sud', *Afrique contemporaine*, 170, 2ème trimestre, (41-46).

Burnell, P., 1994, 'Good Government and Democratization: A Sideway Look at Aid and Political Conditionality', *Democratization*, 1 (3), Fall, (485-503).

Cabanis, A. and Martin, M. L., 1992, 'Notes sur la constitution béninoise du 2 décembre 1990', *Revue juridique et politique*, 46 (1) janvier-mars, (28-37).

* Cadoux, C., 1993, 'La constitution de la troisième République', *Politique africaine*, 52, Madagascar, décembre, (58-66).

Cahen M., 1987, *Mozambique: la révolution imposée: études sur 12 ans d'indépendance (1975-1987)*, Paris, L' Harmattan.

* Cahen, M., 1991, 'Vent des îles: la victoire de l'opposition aux îles du Cap Vert et à Sao Tome et Principe', *Politique africaine*, 43, (63-78).

Cahen M., (ed.), 1994, *Lusotopie: enjeux contemporains dans les espaces lusophones* Paris, Bordeaux, l'Harmattan, CEAN, No. 1-2.

Callaghy, T. M., 1994a, 'Africa's Back to the Future', *Journal of Democracy*, 5(4), October, (133-145).

Callaghy, T. M., 1994b, 'Africa: Falling off the Map?', *Current History*, 93 (579), January, (31-36).

Cammack P., Poll, D., *et al.*, 1993, *Third World Politics: A Comparative Introduction*, London, Macmillan, 320 p.

Campbell, I., 1994, 'Nigeria: the Election that Never Was', *Democratization*, 1 (2), Summer, (309-322).

* Campbell, I., 1994, 'Nigeria's Failed Transition, the 1993 Presidential Elections', *Journal of Contemporary African Studies*, 12 (2), (179-199).

Carew, G. M., 1993, 'Development Theory and the Promise of Democracy in the Future of Post-Colonial African States', *Africa Today*, 40 (4), 1993, (31-53).

Caron, Bernard (ed.), 1992, *Democratic Transition in Africa*, University of Ibadan; Institut français de recherche en Afrique, 436 p.

Carothers T., 1994, 'Democracy and Human Rights: Policy Allies or Rivals?', *Washington Quaterly*, 17 (3), Summer, (109-120).

Carpenter G. and Bewkes M., 1992, 'The Path to Constitutionnal Democracy in South Africa: an Update', *Journal of African Law*, 36(2), Autumn.

Catholic Institute for International Relations, 1993, *Malawi: A Moment of Truth*, London, CIIR, 31 p.

Cawthra, G., 1993, *Policing South Africa: The Sap and the Transition from Apartheid*, London, Zed Books, 240 p.

Chabal, P., 1993a, *Power in Africa: An Essay in Political Interpretation*, London, Macmillan, 311 p.

* Chabal, P., 1993b, 'Some Reflections on the Post Colonial State in Portuguese Speaking Africa', *Africa Insight*, 23 (3), (129-135).

Chakanza, J. C., 1994, 'The Pro-Democracy Movement in Malawi: The Catholic Church's Contribution 1960-1992', *Religion in Malawi*, 4, (8-14).

Chalker, L., 1994, 'The Proper Role of Government', *in* Rimmer D. (ed.), *Action in Africa: The Experience of People in Government Business and Aid*, London, Portsmouth, James Currey, Heinemann, (23-28).

* Champaud, J., 1992, 'Le Sahel et la démocratie', *Politique africaine*, 47, octobre, (3-8).

Champin, C., 1994, 'Malawi: La fin d'un règne', *L'Afrique politique*, 1994: Vue sur la démocratisation à marée basse, (259-268).

Chan, S., 'Democracy in Southern Africa: the 1990's Elections in Zimbabwe and 1991's Elections in Zambia', *Round Table*, 322, April 1992, (183-201).

Charlick, R.B., 'Corruption in Political Transition: A Governance Perspective', *Corruption and Reform*, 7 (3), 1992-93, (177-187).

Charlton, R., 1991, 'Bureaucrats and Politicians in Botswana's Policy Making Process: A Re-Interpretation', *Journal of Commonwealth and Comparative Politics*, 29 (3), (265-282).

* Charlton, R., 1993, 'The Politics of Elections in Botswana', *Africa*, 63 (3), 1993: Understanding Elections in Africa, (330-370).

Chazan, N., 1992, 'Africa's Democratic Challenge: Strengthening Civil Society and the State', in *World Policy Journal*, Spring (279-309).

Chazan, N., 1992, 'Liberalization Governance and Political Space in Ghana', *in* Hyden G. and Bratton M. (eds.), *Governance and Politics in Africa*, Boulder, Lynne Rienner Publishers, 329, (121-141).

Chazan N., Harbeson J. W., *et al.* (eds.), 1993, *Civil Society and the State in Africa*, Boulder, Lynne Rienner Publishers.

Chazan, N., 1993, 'Between Liberalism and Statism: African Political Cultures and Democracy', in Diamond L.J. (ed.), Political Culture and Democracy in Developing Countries Boulder, Lynne Rienner Publishers, 453, (67-108).

Chege, M., 1995, 'Between Africa's Extremes', *Journal of Democracy*, 6 (1), January, (44-51).

Chenu, G. M., 1991, 'La démocratie en Afrique', *Revue juridique et politique, indépendance et coopération*, 1, mars, (6-9).

Cheru, F., 1989, *The Silent Revolution in Africa: Debt, Development and Democracy* London, Harare, Anvil Press, Zed Books, 189 p.

Chhabra, H. S., 1992-1993, 'Democratic South Africa, Prospects', *Africa Quaterly*, 32 (1-4), (81-90).

Chikulo, B. C., 1993, 'End of an Era: An Analysis of the 1991 Zambian Presidential and Parliamentary Elections', *Politikon*, 20 (1), juin.

* Chikulo, B. C., 1994, 'Local Government Reform: The Zambian Case', *Africa Insight*, 24 (4), (133-137).

Chipasuala, J. et Chilvumbo, A. (eds.) 1993, *South Africa's Dilemmas in the Post Apartheid Era*, America University Press, 193 p.

51

* Ciervide, J., 1992, 'Zaïre 1990-1992: éveil du peuple', *Zaïre-Afrique*, 264, (219-226).

* Clapham, C., 1993, 'Democratization in Africa: Obstacles and Prospects', *Third World Quaterly*, 14 (3), 1993, (423-438).

Clark, J. F., 1994a, 'The Constraints on Democracy in Sub-Saharan Africa, The Case for Limited Democracy', *SAIS Review*, 14 (2), Summer-Fall, (91-108).

Clark, J. F., 1994b, 'Elections, Leadership and Democracy in Congo', *Africa Today*, 41(3), (41-60).

Cloete, F., 1992, 'Between Scylla and Charybdis: Policy Choices and the Development of Democracy in South Africa', *in* Vanhanen T. (ed.), *Strategies of Democratization*, Washington, Crane Russak, (143-156).

* Cobbe, J., 1991, 'Lesotho: What Will Happen After Apartheid Goes?', *Africa Today*, 38 (1), (18-32).

Colin, J. P., 1993, 'La démocratie et le tiers monde', *Revue européenne des sciences économiques*, 31(97), (207-223).

Collinge, J. A., 1992, 'Launched on a Bloody Bide: Negociating the New South Africa', *South African Review*, 6, (1-25).

Conac, G., 1991-92, 'Les processus de démocratisation en Afrique', *Parlements et francophonie*, 83-84, (83-95).

* Conac, G., 1992, 'Madagascar, la constitution du 19 août 1992', *Afrique contemporaine*, 166, (56-78).

* Conac, Gérard, (ed.), 1993, *L'Afrique en transition vers le pluralisme politique*, Colloque, Paris, 12-13 décembre 1990, Paris, Economica, 517p.

* Constantin, F. and Quantin, P., 1992, 'Zambie, fin de parti', *Politique africaine*, 45, mars, (123-128).

Coquery-Vidrovitch, C., 1992-93, 'La politique en Afrique noire. Héritage et avenir', Le Genre Humain, 26, Autumn 1992-Winter 1993: Faut-il avoir peur de la démocratie?, 1992-93, (119-140).

* Coulon, C., 1992, 'La démocratie sénégalaise: bilan d'une expérience', *Politique africaine*, 45, mars, *Sénégal: la démocratie à l'épreuve*, (3-8).

Coussy, J., 1995, 'Les rapports ambivalents entre ajustements structurels et démocratie', *Coopération internationale pour la démocratie*, 4, février, (57-70).

Crook, R. C., 1991, 'Decentralisation and Participation in Ghana and Côte d'Ivoire', *in* Crook R.C.and Jerve A.M. (eds.), *Government and Participation: Institutional Development, Decentralisation and Democracy in the Third World*, Bergen, Chr. Michelsen Institute, 219 p, (93-118).

Crook, R. C., 1994, 'Four Years of Ghana District Assemblies in Operation: Decentralization, Democratization and Administrative Performance', *Public Administration and Development*, 14 (4), (339-364).

Crouzel, Y., 1994, 'Afrique du Sud: Le processus de négociation. Qui a franchi le Rubicon?', *L'Afrique politique*, 1994: *Vue sur la démocratisation à marée basse*, (245-258).

Cuddumbey, C., 1995, 'Afrique du Sud: the 1994 Elections', *L'Afrique politique*.

Cullen, C., 1994, *Malawi: A Turning Point*, Edingburgh, Pentland Press.

* Dabezies, P., 1992, 'Vers la démocratisation de l'Afrique', *Défense nationale*, 48 (5), mai (21-33).

Daddah, A., 1994, 'Le fragile pari d'une presse démocratique', *Politique africaine*, 55, octobre 1994: La Mauritanie: un tournant démocratique? (40-55).

Daloz, J.,P., 1992-93, 'Nouvelle République-nouvelle réplique? Velléités transformatrices et perpétuation des comportements politiques au Nigeria', *Année africaine*, (59-88).

Daloz, J. P., 1994, 'Zambie: Analyse d'une dérive prévisible', *L'Afrique politique*, 1994: *Vue sur la démocratisation à marée basse*, (231-244).

Danevad, A., 1993, *Development Planning and the Importance of Democratic Institutions in Botswana*, Bergen, Chr. Michelsen Institute, 171 p.

Danopoulos, C. P., (ed.), 1992, *From Military to Civilan Rule*, London, Routledge, 256p.

Darbon, D., 1992-93, 'In Hac Lacrimarum Valle: Les enjeux précontraints d'une démocratisation cogérée en Afrique du Sud', *Année africaine*, (189-214).

Darbon, D., 1992, 'Afrique du Sud: logiques de destructuration et stratégies ambiguës de reconstruction', *Hérodote*, 65-66, 2-3ème trimestre, (93-112).

Darbon, D., 1994, 'Une transaction démocratique: le miracle de la refondation en Afrique du Sud', *Les Temps modernes*, décembre.

* Darmau, M., 1994, 'Malawi nouveau mais ambigü', *Afrique contemporaine*, 171, 3ème trimestre, (34-35).

Datta, K., 1991, *Democracy and Elections in Botswana with Some Reference to General Litterature on Democracy and Elections in Africa: Bibliography* Talence, CEAN, Bibliographies du CEAN, vol.4, 49 p.

Davidson, A. and Stran, P., 1993, *The Path to Democracy: a Background to the Constitutional Negociations in South Africa*, Uppsala, Uppsala University Press, 119 p.

Davis, D., Hulme, D. and Woodhouse, P., 1994, 'Decentralization by Default: Local Governance and the Views from the Village in the Gambia', *Public Administration and Development*, 14 (3), octobre, (253-269).

De Brito, L., 1994, 'Des élections de paix au Mozambique', *Politique africaine*, 56, décembre, (144-146).

De Gady, Fortman, 1993, 'Conceptualising Democracy in an African Context', *in Democracy and Democratization in Africa*, The Hague, Institute of Social Studies/ Global Coalition for Africa, Final Report, 5, April (9-21).

De Gady. Fortman, 1994, 'Conceptualizing Democracy in African Context', *Quest*, 8(1), June.

De Klerk, W., 1992, 'The Political Process in South Africa', *South Africa International*, 23(3), (65-70).

De Nevers, R., 1993, 'Democratization and Ethnic Conflict', *Survival*, 35 (2), Summer, (31-48).

De Villers, G., 1992, *Zaïre, années 90 (vers la troisième République), volume II: Zaïre 1990-91, faits et dits de la Société d'après le regard de la presse* Bruxelles, CEDAF, Les cahiers du CEDAF, 1-2, 235 p.

Decalo, S., 1992, 'Democracy in Africa: Towards the 21st Century', *in* Vanhanen T. (ed.), *Strategies of Democratization*, Washington, Crane Russak, (131-142).

Decoudras, P. M., 1994, 'Niger: Démocratisation réussie, avenir en suspens', *L'Afrique politique*, 1994: *Vue sur la démocratisation à marée basse*, (45-58).

Decoudras, P. M., Koyt M. and M'Bringa Takama M.F., 1995, 'République Centrafricaine: les vicissitudes du changement', *L'Afrique politique*.

Decraene, P., 1992, 'Réflexions sur l'exigence africaine de démocratisation', *Défense nationale*, (10), octobre, (123-136).

Delbrel, G., 1992, 'Transitions démocratiques: modes et méthodes', *L'Evènement européen*, 19, septembre, (235-248).

Delval, R., 1994, 'Madagascar, de la IIième à la IIIème République', *Revue juridique et politique, indépendance et coopération*, 48 (1), janvier-mars.

Democratization, 1994, 'Political Liberalization and Economic Reform in Africa', Democratization, 1(1), Spring, (100-131).

Deng, L., (ed.), 1991, *Democratization and Structural Adjustment in Africa in the 1990's* Madison, University of Wisconsin-Madison, 215p.

Depelchin, J., 1993, 'Beyond Elite Politics: A Comment on E. Wamba-dia-Wamba's Essay Beyond Elite Politics of Democracy in Africa', *Quest*, 7(1), (100-105).

* Derrick, J., 1992, 'Cameroon: One Party, Many Parties and the State', *African Insight*, 22 (3), (165-177).

Diagoura, M., 1990, 'Demain une Afrique libre', *Echanges et Projets*, 62, décembre 1990: *la démocratisation en Afrique*, (5-8).

Diallo, T. D., 1990, *Gérer la transition démocratique au Mali* Bamako, Imprimeries du Mali, 136p.

Dialogue, 1991, «Démocratie et multipartisme au Rwanda', Dialogue (Kigali), dossier spécial, 144, février, (1-150).

Diamond, L. J., 1991, 'Nigeria's Search for a New Political Order', *Journal of Democracy*, 2 (2), Spring, (54-69).

Diamond L. J. and Marks G. N., 1992, 'Comparative Perspectives on Democracy: Essay in Honor of Seymour Martin Lipset', *American Behavioral Scientist*, 35 (4-5), mars-juin (352-629).

Diamond, L. J. (ed.), 1992a, *The Democratic Revolution: Struggle for Freedom and Pluralism in the Developing World* New York, Freedom House, 254p.

Diamond, L. J., 1992-93, 'Nigeria's Perennial Struggle Against Corruption: Prospects for the Third Republic', *Corruption and Reform*, 7(3), (215-225).

Diamond, L. J., 1992b, 'A Constitution that Works - Some Options', *South Africa International*, 23 (1), (45-48).

* Diop, S., 1992, 'Du parti unique aux multiples partis, ou la démocratie introuvable', *Afrique contemporaine*, Special Issue, 164, octobre-décembre, (145-152).

Diop, S., 1993, 'L'avenir de la démocratie pluraliste en Afrique sub-saharienne', *in* Secrétariat général de la défense nationale (SGDN) (ed), *L'Afrique sub-saharienne: sécurité, stabilité et développement*, 494p., (169-188).

Diouf, A., 1992, 'Sénégal: Vers une réelle démocratie', *Revue des deux mondes*, 10, octobre, (148-153).

* Diouf, M., 1993, 'Les intellectuels africains face à l'entreprise démocratique', *Politique africaine*, 51, octobre, (35-47).

Diouf, M., 1994, 'L'échec du modèle démocratique du Sénégal, 1981-1993', *Afrika Spectrum*, 1, (47-64).

Dodo, A. M. and Laouel Kader, M., 1994, 'Les fondements juridiques de la IIIème République du Niger', *Revue juridique et politique, indépendance et coopération* 1, janvier-mars (71-94).

Doh Shull Shin, 1994, 'On the Third Wave of Democratization: A Synthesis and Evaluation of Recent Theory and Research', *World Politics*, 47 (1), octobre.

Dorraj, M., 1994, 'Privatization, Democratization and Development in the Third World', *Journal of Developing Societies*, 10 (2), July-October 1994, (173-185).

Dosseh-Adjavon, B. A., 1993, *Le Togo en marse vers la démocratie* sl, sn.

Dossou, R. ,1993, 'La transition béninoise', *Parlements et francophonie*, 88-89, avril-juin, (32-36).

Dowden, R., 1993, 'Reflexion on Democracy in Africa', *African Affairs*, 92 (369), October, (607-614).

* Dramé, H., 1993, 'Les défis de l'élection présidentielle en Casamance', *Politique africaine*, 51, octobre (166-169).

Du Bois de Gaudusson, J., 1993, 'L'avenir de la démocratie pluraliste en Afrique, réflexions sur le cas des Etats francophones', in SGDN (ed.), *L'Afrique sub-saharienne, sécurité stabilité et développement*, Paris, La Documentation française, (155-167).

* Duarte, de Carvalho, R., 1995, 'Paix et guerre chez les pasteurs kuvale: lettre de vitivi', *Politique africaine*, 57, (85-93).

Dube, A., 1993, 'State and Society in the Process of Democratization in Africa', *in Democracy and Democratization in Africa*, The Hague, Institute of Social Studies/Global Coalition for Africa, Final Report, 5 April, (61-71).

East, R. and Joseph, T. (eds), 1993, *Political Parties of Africa and the Middle East*, Harlow, Longman, 372p.

Eboh, M. P., 1993, 'Democracy with an African Flair: A Reply to Wamba-dia-Wamba', *Quest*, 7 (1), (92-99).

Eboussi Boulaga, F., 1995, 'Le modèle américain et la démocratisation en Afrique', *Terroirs*, 2, janvier, (18-33).

Eddy, A., 1992, 'La conférence nationale est-elle une solution?', *Parlements et Francophonie*, 25.

Edwards, S. A., 1994, 'Causes of Bewilderment: Necessity, Sufficiency and Facilitating Conditions for Democratization', *Democratization*, 1(3), Fall, (444-460).

Edzodzomo-Ela, M., 1993, *De la démocratie au Gabon: les fondements d'un renouveau national*, Paris, Karthala, 279p.

Egwu, S .G., 1991, 'The Military and the Democratic Quest in Africa', *Nigerian Forum*. 11 (7-8-9), July-September, (166-175).

Ekeh P., 1992, 'The Constitution of Civil Society in African History and Politics', *in* Caron B., Gboyega A. et Osaghae E. (eds.), *Democratic Transition in Africa*, Ibadan, CREDU, Proceeding of a Symposium, 436 p., (187-212).

Elagab, M. Y., 1993, 'The Socio-Economic Conditions for Democracy and Democratization in Africa', *in Democracy and Democratization in Africa*, The Hague, Institute of Social Studies/Global Coalition for Africa, Final Report, 5 April, (22-38).

Elias, N., 1994, 'Burundi: les fruits vénéneux du coup d'Etat', *Politique africaine*, 54, juin, (145-150).

* Ellis, S., 1993, 'Rumour and Power in Togo', *Africa*, 63 (4).

Emery, F. E., 1991, 'What is Real Democracy?' *in* Crook R. C. and Jerve A. M. (eds.), *Government and Participation: Institutional Development, Decentralisation and Democracy in the Third World*, Bergen, Chr. Michelsen Institute, 219 p., (15-20).

Enemuo, F. C., 1992, 'The Resurgence of Multiparty Democracy in Africa: What Hopes for the Downtrodden?', *Nigerian Journal of International Affairs*, 18(2), (26-39).

* Engedayedu, W., 1993, 'Ethiopia: Democracy and the Politics of Ethnicity', *Africa Today*, 40 (2), 2ème trimestre, (29-52).

Engel, U. *et al.* (eds.), 1994, *Wählbeobachtung in Africa: Erfahrungen deutscher Wählbeobachter. Analysen and Lehren Für die Zukunft*, Hamburg, Institut für Afrika Kunde.

* Ergas, Zaki (ed.), 1991, *The African State in Transition*, London: The Macmillan Press, 340p.

* Erpicum, R., A, 1992, 'Dans quelles conditions le milieu rural pourra-t-il participer au processus de démocratisation en Afrique?', *Zaïre-Afrique*, 267, (416-420).

* Esterhuysen, P., 1993, 'Africa in Transition Toward Democracy 1990-93', *Africa Insight*, 23 (4), (198-199).

* Fanomezantsoa, A., 1993, 'Le régicide ambigü ou le mouvement de 1991 vu de Tamatave', *Politique africaine*, 52, décembre.

Fatton, R., 1991, 'Democracy and Civil Society in Africa', *Mediterranean Quarterly*, 2(4), Autumn, (83-95).

* Faure, V., 1992, 'Afrique du Sud: référendum 92, le passage', *Politique africaine*, 46, juin, (126-131).

* Faure, Y., 1993, 'Democracy and Realism: Reflexions on the Case of Côte d'Ivoire', *Africa*, 63 (4), 1993: *Understanding Elections in Africa*, (313-329).

Faure, Y. A., 1991, 'Sur la démocratisation en Côte d'Ivoire: passé et présent', *Année africaine*, (115-160).

Fay, C., 1995, 'La démocratie au Mali, ou le pouvoir en pâture', Cahiers d'études africaines, 35(1), (19-54).

* Ferney, J. C., 1993, 'La France au Rwanda: raison du prince, déraison d'Etat', *Politique africaine*, 51, octobre, Les intellectuels africains, (170-174).

Fernyhough, T., 1993, 'Human Rights and Precolonial Africa', *in* Cohen R., Hyden G., *et al.* (eds.), *Human Rights and Governance in Africa*, Gainesville (ed.), Florida University Press, 312 p. (39-73).

* Forrest, J. B., 1994, 'Namibia: The first Post Apartheid Democracy', *Journal of Democracy*, 5 (3), July 1994, (88-100).

Forsyth, P. and Mare, G., 1992, 'Natal in the New South Africa', *South African Review*, 6, (141-151).

* Founou-Tchuigoua, B.,1994, 'L'occident and la formation d'un potentiel économique de démocratisation dans le Tiers-Monde', *Alternatives Sud*, 1(1), 1994, (45-73).

* Fowler, A., 1993, 'Non Governmental Organizations as Agents of Democratization: An African Perspective', *Journal of International Development*, 5(3), May-June, (325-339).

* Frere, M. S., 1995, 'Pluralisme médiatique au Bénin: l'heure des désillusions?', *Politique Africaine*, 57, mars, (42-149).

Friedman, S., 1992, 'Bonaparte at the Barricades: the Colonisation of Civil Society', *Theoria*, 79, (83-95).

* Friedman, Steven, 1993, 'South Africa's Reluctant Transition', *Journal of Democracy*, Vol. 4, No. 2, April, (56-69).

56

Garang, J. and Khalid, M. (eds.), 1992, *The Call for Democracy in Sudan*, London, Kegan Paul International, 292 p.

Garcin, T., 1992, 'Les européens et la démocratisation africaine', *Afrique 2000*, 10, Juillet-septembre, (19-26).

* Gaud, Michel and Porges, Laurence, 1993, 'Les Présidents de l'Alternance', *Afrique vontemporaine*, No. 167, juillet-septembre, (29-39).

Gaulme, F., 1991, 'Afrique incertaine', *Etudes*, 375 (6), décembre, (581-590).

* Geisler, G., 1993, 'Fair? What has fairness to Do with it? Vagaries of Elections Observations and Democratic Standards', *Journal of Modern African Studies*, 31(4), December, (613-638).

Gerard, J., 1993, 'Elections présidentielles du Sénégal (février 1993): Sopi pour la jeunesse urbaine', *Politique africaine*, 50, juin, (108-114).

* Gerard, J., 1994, 'Un parti vert au Sénégal: une participation militante', *Politique africaine*, 53.

Gervais-Lambony, P., 1994, 'Lomé, troubles politiques et images de la ville', *L'Afrique politique: Vue sur la démocratisation à marée basse* (19-130).

Geschiere, P. and Konings, P., 1993, *Itinéraires d'accumulation au Cameroun*, Paris, Karthala, Leiden, Afrika Studie Centrum, 400 p.

Ghai, Y., 1991, 'The Role of Law in The African Transition of Societies: The African Experience', *Journal of African Law*, 35 (1-2), (8-20).

Ghai, Y., 1992, *Structural Adjustment, Global Interaction and Social Democracy* Genève, U.N. Research Institute for Social Development, Discussion Paper No.37.

Gibbon, P. and Bangura, Y., 1992, *The Social and Political Context of Structural Adjustment*, Uppsala.

Gifford, P., 1994, 'Some Recent Development in African Christianty', *African Affairs*, 93 (373), October, (513-534).

Gilguy, C., 1990, 'Mali: le syndrome béninois', *Géopolitique africaine*, 13 (2), mars, (63-71).

Gilguy, C., 1991, 'Mali: le syndrome ghanéen', *Géopolitique africaine*, 14 (5), octobre-novembre, (1-7).

* Gills, B. and Rocamora J., 1992, 'Low Intensity Democracy', *Third World Quaterly*, 13 (3), 1992, (501-523).

Gills, B., Rocamora, J. and Wilson, R., 1993, *Low Intensity Democracy: Political Power in the New World Order*, London, Pluti Press, 264 p.

Global Coalition for Africa, 1993, *Democracy and Démocratization in Africa*, Washington DC.

Godinec, P., 1993, 'Démocratie et développement en Afrique, perspectives internationales et nationales', *Afrique 2000*, 14, juillet-août, (49-60).

Goga, L., 1991, 'Les ressorts du réveil togolais', *Economie et Humanisme*, 310, décembre, (32-37).

Goldman, R. M., 1990, *From Warfare to Party Politics, The Critical Transition to Civilian Control*, New York, Syracuse University Press, 256p.

* Gonidec, P. F., 1995, 'La crise africaine: une crise d'Etat', *Afrique 2000*, 20 janvier-février-mars, (15-24)

Goodsell, C. T., 1993, 'L'architecture des édifices parlementaires et la culture politique', *Parlements et francophonie,* 90-91, (45-62).

Goumeziane, Smail, 1994, *Le mal algérien: économie politique d'une transition inachevée, 1962-1994,* Paris, Fayard, 307 p.

* Graham, L. S., 1993, 'The Dilemnas of Managing Transition in Weak States: The Case of Mozambique', Public Administration and Development, 13 (4), October.

Grégoire, E. and Labazee, P., 1993, 'Niger: comptes et mécomptes d'un jeune Etat démocratique', *Politique africaine,* 52, décembre, p. 129-131.

* Grégoire, E., 1994, 'Démocratie, Etat et milieux d'affaires au Niger', *Politique africaine,* 56, décembre, p. 94-117.

* Grignon, F., 1993, 'Kenya: l'opposition peut-elle survivre à la défaite?', *Politique africaine,* 52, décembre, (117-121).

Grignon, F., 1993, *Le multipartisme au Kenya? reproduction autoritaire, légitimation et culture politique en mutation, 1990-92,* Nairobi, IFRA, Travaux et documents 12, 81 p.

Grobbelaar, J. Bittereinders, 1992, 'Dilemnas and Dynamics on the Far Right', *South African Review,* 6, (102-111).

Groupe d'études et de recherches sur la démocratie et le développement (s.d.), Recueil *des études du GERDDES,* Cotonou.

* Gruénais, M. E. and Schmitz, J., 1995, 'L'Afrique des pouvoirs et la démocratie', *Cahiers d'études africaines,* 35 (1), (7-18).

* Gruénais, M. E. *et al.,* 1995, 'Messies, fétiches et luttes de pouvoir entre les grands hommes du Congo démocratique', *Cahiers d'études africaines,* 35 (1), (163-174).

Gudina, M., 1994, 'The Ethiopian Transition from Military Authocracy to Popular Democracy?' *Some Major Issues for Consideration in Crossing the Crossroad, Ufahamu,* 22 (1-2).

Gupta, V., 1992-93, 'Violence and Regionalism Delay Democratization', *Africa Quaterly,* 32 (1-4), (107-114).

* Gyimah-Boadi, E., 1994, 'Ghana's Uncertain Political Opening', *Journal of Democracy,* Vol. 5, No. 2, April, (75-86).

Hadenius, A., 1992, *Democracy and Development,* Cambridge, Cambridge University Press, 218 p.

Harir, S., 1993, 'Democracy in Multi-Ethnic Societies: the African Case', *in* Ofstad A. and Wiig A. (eds.), *Development Theory: Recent Trends,* Bergen, Chr. Michelsen Institute, Proceedings of the NFU Annual Conference1992, Report 6, 285 p., (119-134).

Harsh, E., 1993a, 'Structural Adjustment and Africa's Democracy Movements', *Africa Today,* 40 (4), (7-28).

* Harsh, E., 1993b, 'Accumulators and Democrats: Challenging the State Corruption in Africa', *Journal of Modern African Studies,* 31 (1), March (31-48).

Harsh, E., 1993c, 'Structural Adjustment and Africa's Democracy Movements', *Africa Today,* 40 (4), (7-28).

* Hassan, S., 1993, 'The Sudan National Democratic Alliance (NDA): The Quest for Peace, Unity and Democracy', *Issue,* 21 (1-2), 1993: *Toward a New African Political Order, African Perspectives on Democratization Process, Regional Conflict Management,* p.14-26.

58

* Hatchard, J., 1993, 'Re-Establishing a Multy-Parti State: Some Constitutional Lessons from the Seychelles', *Journal of Modern African Studies,* 31 (4), (601-612).

* Haynes, J., 1991, 'Human Rights and Democracy in Ghana, the Record of the Rawling's Regime', *African Affairs,* 90 (360), July.

Haynes, J., 1992, 'One-Party State, No-Party State, Multi-Party State ? 35 Years of Democracy, Authoritarianism and Development in Ghana', in Hugues A. (ed.), *Marxism's Retreat From Africa,* London, Frank Cass & Co, 164 p., (42-62).

* Haynes, J., 1993, 'Sustainable Democracy in Ghana?', *Third World Quaterly,* 14 (3), (451-467).

Hayson, N., 1992, 'Negociating a Political Settlement In South Africa', *South African Review,* 6, (26-43).

* Healey, J., *et al.,* 1993, 'Will Political Reform Bring About Improved Economic Management in Sub-Saharan Africa?', *IDS Bulletin,* 24 (1), (31-38).

* Heilbrunn, J. R., 1993, 'Social Origins of National Conferences in Benin and Togo', *Journal of Modern African Studies,* 31 (2), June, (277-299).

* Helbig, D., 1991, 'Rwanda: de la dictature populaire à la démocratie athénienne', *Politique africaine,* 44, décembre.

Heper, M., 1991, 'Transitions to Democracy Reconsidered: a Historical Perspective', *in* Rustow D.A. et Erickson K.P. (eds.), *Comparative Political Dynamics,* New York, Harper Collins, 495 p., (192-210).

Herholdt, A. N. J., Dombo R. J. and Nel, J. H., 1993, 'Perspectives of Undegraduate Students of the University of the North on the Prospects of the 1994 Elections', *Journal for Contemporary History,* 18 (2), (74-87).

Hillebrand, E., 1993, 'Demokratisierung als Eliten-recycling: das Beispel Gabuns', *Afrika Spectrum,* 28 (1), (73-92).

Holm, J. D., 1992, *Political Culture and Democracy: A Study of Mass Participation in Botswana.* sl, sn, 28 p.

* Holo, T., 1990, 'La transition vers la démocratie: le cas du Bénin', *Alternative démocratique dans le tiers monde,* 2, juillet, (131-169).

* Horowitz, D. L., 1991, *A Democratic South Africa? Constitutional Engineering in a Divided Society,* Berkeley, University of California Press, 293 p.

Horowitz, D. L., 1994, 'Democracy in Divided Societies', *in* Diamond L.J. and Plattner M.F. (eds), *Nationalism, Ethnic Conflict and Democracy,* Baltimore and London, John Hopkins University Press, 146 p., (33-55).

Houngbedji, A., 1994, 'Le renouveau démocratique au Bénin. Genèse, enjeux et perspectives', *Revue juridique et politique, indépendance et coopération,* 1, janvier-mars, (17-26).

Huntington, S., 1991, *The Third Wave: Democratization in the Late Century,* Okhlaoma, Okhlaoma University Press, 336 p.

Huntington, S., 1991-92, 'How Counties Democratize', *Political Science Quarterly,* 106 (4), Winter, (579-616).

Hyden, G., 1991, 'The Role of Aid and Research in the Political Restructuring of Africa', *in* Crook R.C. and Jerve A.M. (eds.), *Government and Participation: Institutional Development, Decentralisation and Democracy in the Third World,* Bergen, Chr. Michelsen Institute, 219 p., (133-158).

Ibeanu, O., 1992, 'Women and Elections in Nigeria: Some Empirical Evidence from the décembre 1991 Elections in Enugu State', *Ufahamu,* 22(2), Spring (64-83).

Ibrahim, J., 1991, *Expanding Democratic Space: an African and Nigerian Discussion,* Zaria, Ahmadu Bello University, 39 p.

Ibrahim, J., 1992, 'From Political Exclusion to Popular Participation: Democratic Transition in Niger', in Caron B., Gboyega A. and Osaghae E. (eds.), *Democratic Transition in Africa,* Ibadan, CREDU, Proceedings of a Symposium, 436 p., (51-68).

Ibrahim, J., 1994, 'Political Exclusion, Democratization and Dynamics of Ethnicity in Niger', *Africa Today,* 41 (3).

Ihonubere, J. O., 1992, 'Is Democracy Possible in Africa? The Elites, The People and Civil Society', Quest, 6(2), (84-108).

Ihonvbere, J. O., 1992, 'The Dynamics of Change in Eastern Europe and their Implications in Africa', *Co-Existence,* 29 (3), September, (277-296).

Ihonvbere, J. O., 1994, *Nigeria: the Politics of Adjustment and Democracy,* New Brunswick and London, Transaction Publishers, 231 p.

Ike, Udogu, E., 1992, 'In Search of Political Stability and Survival: Toward Nigeria's Third Republic', *Scandinavian Journal of Development Alternatives,* 11-(3-4), September-December, (5-28).

Illiassou, A. and Tidjani Alou, M., 1994, 'Processus électoral et démocratisation au Niger', *Politique africaine,* 53, mars, (128-132).

INADES (Institut africain pour le développement économique et social), 1992, *Démocratisation en Afrique, Bibliographie commentée,* Abidjan, INADES Documentation, 58p.

* INADES (Institut africain pour le développement économique et social), 1992,*Démocratie et développement en Afrique,* Abidjan, INADES Formation, Actes du colloque sur Démocratie et développement en Afrique, Bingerville, 20-22 juillet, 51 p.

INADES (Institut Africain pour le Développement Economique et Social), 1994,*Démocratie et développement: bibliographie commentée,* Abidjan, INADES, 29p.

Instituto de Estudos Estrategicos e Internacionals, 1992, *Democratic Reform and Regional Integration: The New Europe and Change in Southern Africa,* Lisbonne, IEEI, Conférence internationale, octobre.

Irung, Tshitambal'a Mulang, 1992, 'La démocratie en Afrique actuelle', *Zaïre-Afrique,* 270, (591-598).

Irung, Tshitambal'a Mulang, 1993, 'L'individu face à la société et la démocratie en Afrique noire traditionnelle', *Zaïre-Afrique,* 272, (71-82).

Irung, Tshitambal'a Mulang, 1993, 'Quelle démocratie pour l'Afrique?', *Zaïre-Afrique,* 279, (527-537).

Irung, Tshitambal, C., 1994, 'Les élections en question', *Zaïre-Afrique,* 34 (287), septembre, (389-402).

Issue, 21 (1-2): *Toward a New African Political Order, African Perspectives on Democratization Process, Regional Conflict Management,* (26-34).

Issue, 1994, 'The News Media and Africa', Special Issue, 22(1), Spring.

Jalade, M., 1991, 'L'évolution économique et institutionnelle du Burkina Faso',*Mondes et Cultures,* 51 (1-2-3-4), (161-166).

Jeffries, R. and Thomas, C., 1993, 'The Ghanaian Elections of 1992', *African Affairs*, 92 (368), July, (331-366).

Jeffries, R., 1993, 'The State, Structural Adjustment and Good Government in Africa', *Journal of Commonwealth and Comparative Politics* 31 (1), March.

* Jewiewicki, B. *et al.*, 1995, 'Du témoignage à l'histoire, des victimes aux martyrs: la naissance de la démocratie à Kinshasa', *Cahiers d'études africaines*, 35 (1), (209-234).

John-Nambo, J., 1994, 'Parodie d'élection présidentielle au Gabon', *Politique africaine*, 53, mars, (33-139).

Johnson, A. *et al.* (eds.), 1993, *Federalism and Constitution Making in the New South Africa*, Leicester, Leicester University Press, 256 p.

* Johnson, A., 1994, 'South Africa: The Election and Transition Process', *Third World Quarterly*, 15 (2), June, (187-204).

Johnson, Walton R., 1994, *Dismantling Apartheid: A South African Town in Transition*, Cornell University Press, 272 p.

Johnston, M., 1992-93, 'Micro and Macro Possibilities for Reform', *Corruption and Reform*, 7 (3), 1992-93, (189-204).

Joseph, R., 1993, 'The Christian Churches and Democracy in Contemporary Africa', *in* White J. (ed.), *Christianity and Democracy in a Global Context*, Boulder, Lynne Rienner Publishers.

Journal of Commonwealth and Comparative Politics 30 (3), November, (316-334).

Kafureeka, L., 1993, 'Multi Party Movement in Africa: A Defi for Democracy', in *Democracy and Democratization in Africa* The Hague, Institute of Social Studies/ Global Coalition for Africa, Report, 5 April, (89-105).

Kala-Lobe, S., 1990, 'La nécessaire révolution culturelle', *Echanges et Projets*, 62, *La démocratisation en Afrique*, décembre, (17-23).

Kalambaye, E., 1991, 'Démocratie et multipartisme: la responsabilité de l'intellectuel africain', *Afrique 2000*, 5, mai, (55-58).

Kalfleche, J. M., 1991, 'Premier handicap de la démocratisation: l'indétermination de l'Europe', *Géopolitique africaine*, 14 (3) mai-juin, (3-14).

Kamanga, K., 1993, 'The Malawi Republic Constitution and Multi-Partyism Main Concerns', *Verfassung und Recht in Übersee*, 26 (3), (245-257).

* Kamto, M., 1994, 'Les rapports Etat-société civile en Afrique', *Afrique 2000*, 19, octobre-décember, (47-52).

Kamto, M., 1994, 'Les rapports Etat-société civile en Afrique', *Revue juridique et politique, indépendance et coopération*, 3, octobre-décembre, (285-291).

* Kante, B., 1994, 'Senegal's Empty Elections', *Journal of Democracy*, 5 (1), January, (96-108).

Kaphagawani, D. N., 1993, 'Democratic Practice in Africa. Some Arguments', *Quest*, 7 (2), December.

* Kaplinsky, R., 1994, 'A Policy Agenda for Post-Apartheid South Africa', *IDS Bulletin*, 25 (1), (73).

Karikari, K., 1993, 'Africa: The Press and Democracy', *Race and Class*, 34 (3).

Kasereka, K., 1994, 'Afrique et démocratie: quel nouvel ordre du discours?', *Zaïre-Afrique*, 284, avril, (207-223).

Kasfir, N., 1992, 'Popular Sovereignty and Popular Participation: Mixed Constitutionnal Democracy in the Third World', *Third World Quaterly*, 13 (4), (587-605).

* Kasse, M., 1990, 'Démocratie et développement en Afrique', *Alternative démocratique dans le tiers monde*, 2, juillet-décembre, (95-103).

Kawonise, S., 1992, 'Normative Impediments to Democratic Transition in Africa', in Caron B., Gboyega A. & Osaghae E. (eds.), *Democratic Transition in Africa*, Ibadan, CREDU, Proceedings of a Symposium, 436 p., (129-140).

Keller, E. J., 1991, 'The State in Contemporary Africa: A Critical Assessment of Theory and Practice', in Rustow D.A. and Erickson K.P. (eds.), *Comparative Political Dynamics*, New York, Harper Collins, 495 p., (134-160).

* Keller, E. J., 1993, 'Toward a New African Order?', *Africa Insight*, 23 (3), (124-128).

* Kempton, D. R., 1991, 'Africa in the Age of Perestroïka', *Africa Today*, 38 (2), (7-29).

Kempton, D. R. and Mosia, L., 1992, 'The International Community in South Africa's Transition to Non Racial Democracy', *International Affairs Bulletin*, 16 (2), (5-31).

Kendall, F., 1991, *The Heart of the Nation: Regional and Community Government in the New South Africa*, Norwood, Amagi, 196 p.

Khadiagala, G. M., 1992, 'Thoughts on Africa and the New World Order', *Round Table*, 324, October, (431-450).

Khagram, S., 1993, 'Democracy and Democratization in Africa: A Plea for Pragmatic Possibilism', *Africa Today*, 40 (4), 1993, (55-74).

Khalil, M. I., 1994, 'Sudan's Democratic Experiment: Present Crisis and Future Prospects', *North East African Studies*, 1 (2-3).

Kihoro, W., 1992, 'Politics and Democracy in Kenya', in Londsdale J. (ed.), *Politics in Kenya*, Edingburg, Centre of African Studies.

* Kinkela, Vi Kans'y, 1993, 'Rapport final des travaux de la Conférence nationale souveraine', *Zaïre-Afrique*, 273, (135-199).

* Kirk, Greene, A. H. M., 1991, 'His Eternity, His Eccentricity or His Exemplarity? A Further Contribution to the Study of H.E. the African Head of State', *African Affairs*, 90 (359), April (163-187).

* Kirongozi, B. L., 1994, 'De l'Etat patriarchique à Etat de droit: essai de clarification de la problématique de l'Etat en Afrique noire', *Afrique 2000*, octobre-décembre, (105-122).

Kock, C. D. and Schutte, C., 1993, 'Factors Contributiong to Violence Before, During and After the Election of an Interim/Transitional Government in South Africa', *Strategic Review for Southern Africa*, 15 (2), November, (1-42).

Kodjo, E., 1991, *Démocratisation en Afrique*, Talence, CEAN, Conférence, IEP de Bordeaux, 6 février, Cassette vidéo 2h22 p.

Kodjo, E., 1992, 1992, 'Le nouvel ordre mondial et l'Afrique', *Afrique 2000*, 10, juillet-septembre, (5-17).

* Kodmani-Darwish, Bassma; Chartouni-Dubarry, mai, (eds.), 1990, *Maghreb: les Années de Transition*, Paris, Masson, 399p.

* Korn, A., 1993, 'Intellectuels africains et enjeux de la démocratie: misère, répression et exil', *Politique africaine*, 51, octobre, (61-67).

Kombila, Iboanga F., 1991, 'La résistance du pouvoir à l'instauration de la démocratie pluraliste en Afrique: le cas du Gabon' *Revue juridique et politique, indépendance et coopération,* 45 (1), (10-23).

Kombila, Iboanga F., 1991, 'A propos de la pratique récente de la conférence nationale en Afrique noire, à la lumière de la conférence nationale gabonnaise: une nouvelle forme de déclaration des droits?', *Revue juridique et politique, indépendance et coopération,* 45 (3-4), (267-281).

Kotze, H., 1991, *Elites and Democratization: An Explanatory Survey of South African Studies,* Stellenbosch, Center for South African Politics, Occasional Paper 1, 100p.

Kouassi, E. K., 1993, 'Reflexions sur la constitution togolaise de la IVème République (le renouveau démocratique)', *Revue congolaise de droit,* 11-12-13-14, janvier 1992.

Kouassi, E. K., 1994, 'La réforme de l'administration territoriale au Niger', *Revue Congolaise de Droit,* 15-16, janvier-décembre, (37-50).

Kourliandsky, J. J., 1994, 'Les démocraties de basse intensité', *Relations internationales et stratégiques,* 14, Summer, (45-151).

Koutoudi, I., 1993, *Transition à la nigérienne: récit,* Niamey, Nouvelle imprimerie du Niger.

Kpundeh, S. J. and Riley, S. P., 1992, 'Political Choice and the New Democratic Politics in Africa', *Round Table,* 323, July, (263-271).

Kpundeh, S. J., 1992, *Democratization in Africa: African Views, African Voices. Summary of Three Workshop,* Washington DC, National Academy Press, 85p.

Krieger, M., 1994, 'Cameroon's Democratic Crossroads, 1990-94', *Journal of Modern African Studies,* 32 (4), December, (605-628).

Kufuor, K. O., 1993, 'The Limits of Human Rights: Some Aspects of the Ghanian 4th Republican Constitution', *Verfassung Recht in Übersee,* 26 (4), (362-371).

* Kunz, F. A., 1991, 'Liberalization in Africa: Some Preliminary Reflections', *African Affairs,* 90 (359), April.

Labertit, G., 1994, 'L'Afrique et la démocratie: la fin d'un apartheid planétaire', *Relations internationales et stratégiques,* 14, Summer, (110-118).

Lafargue, J., 1994, 'Zambie vers une démocratie lacunaire?', *Politique africaine,* 54, juin, (150-156).

* Lancaster, C., 1993, 'Governance and Development: The Views from Washington', *IDS Bulletin,* 24 (1), (9-15).

Lancaster, C., 1993, 'Democratization in Sub-Saharan Africa', *Survival,* 35 (3), Fall (38-50).

* Landell-Mills, P., 1992, 'Governance, Cultural Change and Empowerment', *Journal of Modern African Studies,* 30 (4).

Lapoulo, F., 1993, 'La conférence nationale au Bénin: un concept nouveau de changement de régime politique', *Année africaine,* (89-114).

* Le Bris, E. and Quantin, P., 1992, 'Les barricades, sont-elles anti-constitutionnelles?', *Politique africaine,* 49 décembre, (142-146).

Le Courrier, 1993, 'Afrique: les nouvelles démocraties', *Le Courrier,* dossier spécial, 138, mars-avril, (62-88).

* Le Roy, E., 1992, 'Le Mali: la troisième République face à la méfiance des ruraux', *Politique africaine,* 46, juin, (138-142).

Le Vine, V. T., 1992-93, 'Administrative Corruption and Democratization in Africa: Aspects of the Theoretic Agenda', *Corruption and Reform*, 7 (3), (271-278).

* Lee, Robin and Schlemmer, Lawrence, (eds.), 1991, *Transition to Democracy: Policy Perspectives 1991: Contemporary South African Debates,* Cape Town, Oxford University Press, 278p.

* Leftwich, A., 1993, 'Governance, Democracy and Development in the Third World', *Third World Quarterly*, 14 (3), (605-624).

Lelart, M., 1992, 'Le Fond monétaire international et la démocratie', *Trimestre du monde*, 1st Quarter, (91-104).

* Lemarchand, R., 1992a, 'Uncivil States and Civil Societies: How Ilusion Became Reality', *Journal of Modern African Studies*, 30 (2), (177-191).

* Lemarchand, René, 1992b, 'Africa's Troubled Transitions', *Journal of Democracy*, Vol. 3, No. 4, October, (98-109).

Lemarchand, R., 1994, 'Managing Transitions Anarchies: Rwanda, Burundi and South Africa in Comparative Perspective', *Journal of Modern African Studies*, 32 (4), décembre, (581-604).

Les cahiers du CEDAF -(5-6), vol.1, (24 avril 1990-22 septembre 1991),

Lewis, B., 1993, *Islam et démocratie*, Paris, Fondation Saint-Simon, 31p.

Lewis, P. M., 1994, 'Endgame in Nigeria ? The Politics of a Failed Democratic Transition', *African Affairs*, 93 (372), July, (323-340).

Leymarie, P., 1993, 'Les militaires africains face à l'explosion démocratique', *Le Monde diplomatique*, mars.

Ligunya A. A., 1994, 'The African Woman and Democratization Process', in *Democracy and Democratization in Africa,* Enschede, International Institute for Aerospace Survey and Earth Science/Global Coalition for Africa, Final Report, 18-19 March, 92 p., (66-67).

Lindeke, W. A. and Wanzala, W., 1994, 'Regional Elections in Namibia. Deepening Democracy and the Gender Inclusion', *Africa Today*, 41 (3), (5-14).

* Lipset, S. M.; Seong, K. R. and Torres, J. C., 1993, 'Une analyse comparative des prérequis sociaux de la démocratie', *Revue internationale des sciences sociales*, 136, mai, (181-215).

Lipumba, N. H. I. and Mbelle, A. V. Y., 1993, 'Policy Making for Economic Growth and Poverty Elimination in a Pluralistic System in Tanzania. An Overview', *in* Bagachwa M.S.D. and Mbelle A.V.Y. (eds*), Economic Policy under a Multiparty System in Tanzania*, Dar-es-Salaam, Dar-es-Salaam University Press.

Loada, A. M. G., 1995, 'Burkina Faso: les rentes de la légitimation démocratique', *L'Afrique politique*.

Lonsdale, J. and Kihoro, W., 1992, *Politics in Kenya*, Edinbourg, Centre of African Studies, Occasional Papers 37, 34 p.

* Lootvoet, B. and Ecoutin, J. M., 1993, 'Les maux de la presse écrite guinéenne', *Politique africaine*, 51, octobre.

* Luckham, R., 1994, 'The Military, Militarization and Democratization in Africa: A Survey of Literature and Issues', *The African Studies Review*, 37 (2), September, (13-76).

M'Ba, 1992, 1992, 'Quels hommes pour conduire la transition démocratique', *Afrique 2000*, 10, juillet-septembre, (57-66).

M'Bokolo, E., 1990, 'Obstacles et risques de dérive', 1990, *Echanges et Projets*, numéro special sur 'La démocratisation en Afrique', 62, décembre, (25-31).

M'Nteba, M., 1992, 'Afrique: à quand la fin des indépendances?', *Etudes*, 376 (6), juin, (725-732).

* Maake, N. P.,1992, 'Multi-cultural Relations in a Post-Apartheid South Africa', *African Affairs*, 91 (365), (583-604).

Mabeko-Tali, J.M., 1993, *Les bacongo et la transition démocratique en Angola: démocratie ou représentation ethnico-régionale?*, Paris, sn.

* MacDonald, M., 1992, 'The Sirens Song: the Political Logic of Power Sharing in South Africa (A Critique of Arend Lijphart and Donald Horowitz)', Journal of Southern African Studies, 18 (4), (709-725).

* Madisa, M., 1991, *Democracy in Botswana*, Harare, SAPES, State and Democracy, 2, 63p.

Mahmud, S., 1993 'The Failed Transition to Civilian Rule in Nigeria: Its Implications for Democracy and Human Rights', *Africa Today*, 40 (4), (87-95).

Maidoka, A., 1993, 'La constitution nigérienne du 26 décembe 1992', *Revue juridique et politique, indépendance et coopération*, 47 (3), septembre, (475-491).

Mair, S., 1993, *Kenias Weg in die Mehrparteien Demokratie. Ursachen, Akteure und Interessen*, Ebenhausen, Stiftung Wisanschaft und Politik.

Makassy, G., 1995, 'La constitution congolaise du 15 mars 1992', *Revue juridique et politique*, janvier-avril.

* Makebo, Tali, J. M., 1995, 'La chasse aux zaïrois à Luanda', *Politique africaine*, 57, mars, (71-84).

Malanda, A. S., 1994, 'Démocratie et violence en Afrique', *Revue des deux mondes*, 11, novembre, (129-137).

Mallaby, S., 1992, *After Apartheid*, London, Faber & Faber, 210p.

Mallarde, E., 1990, 'Congo: une chance à saisir', *Géopolitique africaine*, mars, (39-48).

* Mane, Ibrahima, (ed.), 1996, *Etat, démocratie, sociétés et culture en Afrique*, Dakar, Editions démocraties africaines.

Manga, P., 1994, 'Réflexion sur la dynamique constitutionnelle en Afrique', *Revue juridique et politique, Indépendance et coopération*, 1, janvier-mars, (46-70).

Maniruzzaman, T., 1987, *Military Withdrawal from Politics*, Cambridge, Ballinger Publishing Company, 250p.

* Maphai, V., 1993, 'Prospects for a Democratic South Africa', *African Affairs*, 69 (2) avril, *Africa and Democracy*, (223-238).

* Marchal, R., 1993, 'Erythrée an 01', *Politique africaine*, 50, juin, (21-31).

Marsesin, P., 1994, 'Origine et évolution des partis et groupes politiques', *Politique africaine*, 55, octobre: *La Mauritanie: un tournant démocratique?*, (20-30).

Marshall, J., 1993, *Literacy, Power and Democracy in Mozambique*, Boulder, Westview Press.

* Martin, D. C., 1993, 'La Tanzanie et le Multipartisme', *Afrique contemporaine*, 167, (3-13).

Massina, P., 1993, 'De la souveraineté des Conférences nationales africaines', *Revue burkinabe de droit*, 24, décembre.

Matlosa, K., 1992, 'Multi-partism vs Democracy in Southern Africa: Wither Lesotho', *Verfassung und Recht in Übersee,* 25 (3), (327-340).

Mattes, R. B., 1992, *The Myths of Majoritarianism: Understanding Democracy in a New South Africa,* Mowbray, Idasa, Occasional Paper 43, 6p.

Mavila, J. C., 'L'Etat africain, quelles perspectives de changement des institutions?', *Revue congolaise de droit,* 11-12-13-14, janvier 1992-décembre 1993.

Mawhood, P., 1991, 'The Politics of Decentralisation: Eastern Europe and Africa', in Crook R.C. and Jerve A.M. (eds.), *Government and Participation: Institutional Development, Decentralisation and Democracy in the Third World,* Bergen, Chr. Michelsen Institute, 219 p., (51-68).

Mazrui, A., 1993, 'Ethinicity and Pluralism: The politization of Religion in Kenya', *Journal Institute of Muslim Minority Affairs,* 14 (1-2), January-July, (191-201).

Mbachu, O., 1992, 'The Impact or Perestroïka and Glastmost on African Politics', *Co-Existence,* 29 (3), September, (297-304).

Mbachu, O., 1992, 'Democracy and the Rule of Law: A Case Study of Nigeria', Indian Journal of Political Science, 53 (3), July-September, (374-396).

Mbaku, J. M., 1994, 'Rent Seeking and Democratization Strategies for Africa', *International Afrika Forum,* 30 (3).

Mbembe, A., 1992, 'L'ère des transitions', *Belvédère,* 4 (1294), janvier-février, (48-51).

Mbembe, A., 1993, 'Déconfiture de l'Etat et risques de la transition démocratique', *Le Monde diplomatique,* Mai.

* Mbembe, Achille, 1993, 'Diagnostic sur les dérapages de la transition démocratique en Afrique', *Afrique 2000,* 12, janvier-février-mars, (57-63).

Mbu, N. A. T., 1993, *Civil Disobedience in Cameroun,* Bamenda, s.n.

McFerson, H., 1992, 'Democracy and Development in Africa', *Journal of Peace Research,* 24 (3), (241-248).

McLean, I., 1994, 'Democratization and Economic Liberalization: Which is the Chicken and Which is the Egg?', *Democratisation,* 1 (1), Spring, (27-40).

Médard, J. F., 1993, 'L'africanisation du modèle occidental d'Etat', in SGDN (Secrétariat général de la défense nationale) (ed.), *L'Afrique subsaharienne: sécurité, stabilité et développement,* 494 p., (p. 139-153).

* Medhanie, Testfasion, 1993, 'Les Modèles de Transition Démocratique', *Afrique 2000,* No. 14, juillet-August-septembre, (61-69).

Mehler, A., 1993, *Kamerun in der Ära Biya: Bedingungen erste Schritte und Blochaden einer democratischer Transition,* Hamburg, Institut für Afrika Kunde.

Mekongo, L. E., 1990, 'Après le déshonneur, quels lendemains pour l'Afrique?' *Echanges et Projets,* 62, La démocratisation en Afrique, décembre, (9-15).

Meledje, Djedjro, F., 1992, 'La révision des constitutions dans les Etats africains francophones', *Revue du droit public et de la science politique en France et l'étranger,* 108 (1), février, (111-134).

Mendes-Fernandes, R., 1994, 'Guinée-Bissau: Transition démocratique?' *L'Afrique politique,* Vue sur la démocratisation à marée basse, p. 81-92.

* Menga, Guy, 1993, *Congo: La transition escamotée,* Paris, L'Harmattan, 217p.

* Mengue, Me Engouang. F., 1990, 'La transition vers la démocratie pluraliste, l'exemple du Gabon', *Alternative démocratique dans le tiers monde*, 2, juillet-décembre, (171-176).

Messiant, C., 1994, 'Angola: Le retour à la guerre, ou l'inavouable faillite d'une intervention internationale', *L'Afrique politique: Vue sur la démocratisation à marée basse*, (199-230).

* Messiant, C., 1995, 'MPLA et UNITA: processus de paix et logique de guerre', *Politique africaine*, 57, mars, (40-57).

* Metena, M'Teba., 1993, 'Les conférences nationales africaines and la figure de l'évêque-président', *Zaïre-Afrique*, 276, p. 361-372.

Meyns, P., 1992-93, 'Civil Society and Democratic Change in Africa. The Case of Cape Verde and Zambie', *Africa Development Perspectives Yearbook*, 3.

Michaels, M., 1993, 'Retreat from Africa', *Foreign Affairs*, 72 (1).

Michalon, T., 1995, 'L'Etat africain: quête d'une nouvelle légitimité', *Terroirs*, 2, janvier, (5-17).

Mkhondo, R., 1993, *Reporting South Africa*, London, Portmouth, J. Currey, Heinemann, 194p.

Mmuya, M. and Ghaligha, A., 1992, *Towards Multiparty Politics in Tanzania: A Spectrum of the Current Opposition and the CCM Response*, Dar es Salam, Friedrich Ebert Stiftung/Dar-es-Salaam University Press, VII + 167 p.

Mohs, R. M. and Repnik, H. P., 1992, 'Good Governance, Democracy and Development Paradigms', *Intereconomics*, 17 (1), January, (28-33).

* Molutsi P. and Holm, J. D., 1990, 'Developing Democracy When Civil Society is Weak: the Case of Botswana', *African Affairs*, 89 (356), July, (323-340).

* Molutsi, P., 1991, *International Influences on Botswana Democracy*, Washington, John Hopkins University Press, 24 p.

* Molutsi, P. P., 1991a, 'Political Parties and Democracy in Botswana', *in* Molomo M.G. and Mokopakgosi B.T. (eds.) *Multi-Party Democracy in Botswana*, Harare, SAPES, State and Democracy, 2, 63 p., (5-9).

* Molutsi, P. P., 1991b, 'The Political Economy of Botswana: Implications for Democracy', in Molomo M.G. and Mokopakgosi B.T. (eds.), *Multi-Party Democracy in Botswana*, Harare, SAPES, State and Democracy, 2, 63 p., (29-37).

* Momolo, M .G., 1991, 'Botswana's Political Process', *in* Molomo M.G. and Mokopakgosi B.T. (eds.), Multi-Party Democracy in Botswana, Harare, SAPES, State and Democracy, 2, 63 p., (11-22).

Monga, C., 1991, 'L'émergence de nouveaux modes de production démocratique en Afrique noire', *Afrique 2000*, 7 novembre, (11-125).

Monga, C., 1994, *Anthropologie de la colère (société civile et démocratie en Afrique noire)*, Paris, l'Harmattan, 167 p.

Monkotan, K. J. B., 1991, 'Une nouvelle voie d'accès au pluralisme politique: la Conférence nationale souveraine', *Afrique 2000*, 7 octobre-décembre, (41-55).

Monnier, L., 1992, 'Démocratie et développement en Afrique noire: quels termes pour le débats?', *Informations et commentaires*, 78, janvier-mars, (27-32).

Monnier, L., 1993, 'Démocratie et faction en Afrique centrale', *Revue nouvelle*, 86 (1-2), janvier-février, (122-131).

* Monsengwo, Pasinyia, L., 1993, 'La démocratisation au Zaïre et ses protagonistes', *Zaïre-Afrique*, 275, (275-285).

Moore, M. and Hamalai, L., 1993, *Economic Liberalization, Political Pluralism and Business Associations in Developping Countries*, Brighton, Institute of Development Studies, IDS Discussion Papers, 318, 47 p.

Moran, M. and Parry, G. (eds.), 1994, *Democracy and Democratization*, London, Routledge, 298 p.

Morel, Y., 1992, 'Démocratisation en Afrique noire, les Conférences nationales', *Etudes*, 376 (6) juin, (733-743).

Moris, M. and Hindson, D., 1992, 'The Desintegration of Apartheid: From Violence to Reconstruction', *South African Review*, 6, (152-170).

* Morrison, J. Stephen, 1992, 'Ethiopia Charts a New Course', *Journal of Democracy*, Vol. 3, No. 3, July, (125-137).

Moss, T. O., 1992, 'La conditionnalité démocratique dans les relations entre l'Europe et l'Afrique', *L'Evènement européen*, 19, septembre, (225-234).

Motlhabi, M., 1992, *Toward a New South Africa: Issues and Objects in the ANC/Government Negociations for a Non Racial Democratic Society* Skotaville, Braamfontein, 88 p.

Mouddour, B., 1992, 'La fin d'un mythe: l'avènement du multipartisme en Afrique', *Revue juridique et politique, indépendance et coopération*, 46 (1), 1992, (38-45).

Mouelle, Kombi II, N., 1991, 'La conférence nationale africaine: l'émergence d'un mythe politique', *Afrique 2000*, 7 novembre, (35-40).

* Mouelle, Kombi II, N., 1994, 'Consultation électorale et respect de l'expression des citoyens', *Afrique 2000*, 16, janvier-mars, (41-50).

* Mougel, P., 1993, 'Lesotho: retour à la démocratie', *Politique africaine*, 51, octobre, pp. 175-178.

* Moukoko, Mbonjo, Pierre, 1993, 'Régimes militaires et transition démocratique en Afrique: à la recherche d'un cadre d'analyse théorique', *Afrique 2000*, 13, avril-mai-juin, (39-58).

* Moukoko, Mbonjo, P., 1993, 'Pluralisme socio-politique et démocratie en Afrique: l'approche consociationnelle ou du Power Sharing', *Afrique 2000*, 15 octobre-décembre, (39-54).

Moukoko, Priso, 1994, *Cameroun = Kamerun: la transition dans l'impasse*, Paris, Ed. l'Harmattan.

Moyo, J. N., 1991, 'Democracy in the Africa Reality: Policy Relevance of Leftist Intellectual', *Africa Quarterly*, 31 (1-2), (47-58).

Moyo, J. N., 1993, 'Civil Society in Zimbabwe', *Zambezia*, 20 (1), (1-13).

* Mpati, Ne Nzita, N., 'L'épiscopat zaïrois face à la démocratie naissante au Zaïre', *Zaïre-Afrique*, 265, (268-274).

* Mubiala, M., 1994, 'L'aide à la démocratie', *Afrique 2000*, 17 avril-juin, (27-34).

* Muigai, G., 1993, 'Kenya's Opposition and the Crisis of Governance'.

Munck, G. L., 1994, 'Democratic Transition in Comparative Perspective', *Comparative Politics*, 26 (3), April, (355-375).

Munslow, B., 1993, 'Democratization in Africa', *Parliamentary Affairs*, 46 (4), October, (478-490).

Museveni, Y. K., 1994, 'Democracy and Good Governance in Africa: An African Perspective', *Mediterranean Quarterly*, 5 (4), Autumn, (1-8).

Mutahaba, G. R., 1991, 'Organisation for Local Governance: Searching for an Appropriate Local Level Institutional Framework in Tanzania', *in* Crook R.C. and Jerve A.M. (eds.), *Government and Participation: Institutional Development. Decentralisation and Democracy in the Third World*, Bergen, Chr. Michelsen Institute, 219 p., (69-92).

Nambo, J. J., 1994, 'Parodie d'élection présidentielle au Gabon', *Politique africaine*, 53, mars, (133- 138).

* Nana, Sinkam, S. C., 1993, 'Démocratie et développement en Afrique: peut-on les réussir?', *Afrique 2000*, 14, (71-82).

* Nana, Sinkam, S. C., 1994, 'L'Afrique: la transition économique et démocratique', *Afrique 2000*, 16, janvier-mars, (51-66).

Nannan, S. S., 1992, 'Africa: The Move Toward Democracy', *Strategic Analysis*, 14 (10), January, (221-1232).

National Democratic Institute for International Affairs, 1992, *An Evaluation of the June 21 1992 Elections in Ethiopia*, Washington DC, X + 159 p., Issue, 1994, 'The News Media and Africa', *Issue*, Spécial Issue, 22 (1), Spring.

National Democratic Institute for International Affairs, 1992, *Une évaluation des élections du 11 octobre 1992*, Washington DC, IX + 129 p.

National Democratic Institute for International Affairs/Carter Center of Emery University, 1992, *The octobre 31, 1991 National Elections in Zambia*, Washington DC, 167 p.

Ndiaye, B., 1990, 'Développement économique et démocratie en Afrique', *African Development Review*, 2 (2), décembre, (49-57).

Ndiaye, T. M., 1992, 'Des transitions démocratiques en Afrique', *Alternative démocratique dans le tiers monde*, 6, juillet-décembre, (13-29).

* Ndue, P. N., 1994, 'Africa's Turn Toward Pluralism', *Journal of Democracy*, 5 (1), January.

Neocosmos, M., 1994, 'Lesotho: Political Liberalization: Recent Developments', *L'Afrique Politique. Vue sur la démocratisation à marée basse*, (269-280).

Newbury, C., 1994, 'Paradoxes of Democratization in Africa', *The African Studies Review*, 37 (1), April, (1-8).

Ngcobo, L., 1991, 'Impressions and Thoughts on the Options of South African Women', *Kunapipi*, 13 (1-2), (165-169).

Ngniman, Z., 1993, *Cameroun: la démocratie emballée*, Yaoundé, Clé, 315 p.

Ngolongolo, A. (ed.), 1993, *Congo, bravo ou fiasco ? depuis la conférence nationale*, Champigny/Marne, 210 p.

Nguema, I., 1990, *Democratie gabonaise: droits de l'homme et développement: intervention à la conférence nationale sur la démocratie et le multipartisme*, Libreville 23 mars-11 avril, s.n., 13 p.

Nguema, I., 1992, 'La démocratie, l'Afrque traditionnelle et le développement', *Afrique 2000*, 10, juillet-septembre (27-56).

Niandou, Souley, A., 1990-91, 'Tracts et démocratisation au Niger', *Année africaine*, 1990-91, (431).

Niandou, Souley, A., 1992, 'Crise des autoritarismes militaires et renouveau politique en Afrique de l'ouest: étude comparative', Bénin, Mali, Niger, Togo, Université Bordeaux I, thèse, Science politique, 431 p.

Niandou, Souley, 1992, 'Economic Crisis and Democratization in Africa', in Caron B. Gboyega A. And Osaghae E. (eds.) *Democratic Transition in Africa*, Ibadan, CREDU, Proceedings of a Symposium, 436 p., (379-385).

Nolutshungu, S. C., 1992, 'Africa in a World of Democracies: Interpretation and Retrieval',

Nolutshungu, S. C., 1992, 'Reflections on National Unity in South Africa: A Comparative Approach'', *Third World Quarterly*, 13 (4), (607-625).

Novello, G. Sulle, 1991, 'Società post communiste al di fuori dell'Europa: il caso del Benin', *Affari Sociali Internazionali*, 19 (3), (16-28).

Nwabueze, B. O., 1992, *Military Rule and Constitutionnalism in Nigeria*, Ibadan, Spectrum Books, 368 p.

Nwajiaku, K., 1993, 'An Exploration of the Democratization ProcessThrough the Medium of the Conference Nationale in Benin and Togo', London, Master of Arts in Area Studies, Africa, 60 p.

Nwankwo, A. A. 1993, *Nigeria: The Political Transition and the Future of Democracy* Enugu, Fourth Dimension, 223 p.

Nwokedi, E., 1990, 'Mandela and the Transition to a Post-Apartheid South Africa',*Nigerian Forum*, 10 (3-4), pp. 71-79.

Nwokedi, E., 1993, 'Democratic Transition and Democratization in Francophone Africa', *Verfassung und Recht in übersee*, 26 (4), p. 399-436

Nwokedi, E., 1993, *Civil Society and Democratic Transition in Africa: the Mechanism of the National Conference* Bremen, IZA, Afrika Diskussions Papiere, 2, 18 p.

Nwokedi, E., 1994, 'Nigeria's Democratic Transition: Explaining the Annulled 1993 Presidential Election', *Round Table*, 330, avril, p. 189-204.

* Nyang'Oro, J. E., 1993, 'Democracy and NGO's in Africa',*Scandinavian Journal of Development Alternatives*, 12 (2-3), pp. 277-291.

Nyang'Oro, J. E., 1994, 'Reform Politics and Democratization Process in Africa',*The African Studies Review*, 37 (1), April, p. 133-146.

Nyeme, Tese, J. A.,1994, 'L'apport des églises à la démocratisation en Afrique', *Zaïre-Afrique*, 284, avril.

Nzimande, B. and Sikhosana, M., 1992, 'Civil Society and Democracy',*African Communist*, *128*, 1st Quater, p. 37-51.

* Nzouankeu, J. M., 1991, 'Démocratie majoritaire et démocratie concensuelle',*Actualité de la démocratie dans le tiers monde*, 1, juillet-décembre, pp. 5-17.

* Nzouankeu, J. M., 1991, 'L'Afrique devant l'idée de démocratie',*Revue internationale des sciences sociales*, 128, mai, pp. 397-409.

* Nzouankeu, J. M., 1992, 'La transition démocratique au Mali',*Alternative démocratique dans le tiers monde*, 3-4-5, janvier 1991-juin 1992, pp. 123-316.

Nzouankeu, J. M., 1993, 'The Role of the National Conference in the Transition to Democracy in Africa: The Cases of Benin and Mali', *Issue*, 21 (1-2): *Toward a New African Political Order, African Perpectives on Democratization Process, Regional Conflict Management*, pp. 44-50.

Nzouankeu, J. M., 1994, 'Décentralisation et démocratie en Afrique', *Revue internationale des sciences administratives*, 60 (2), juin, p. 255-270.

Nzuzi, L., 1995, 'Zaïre: Bilan quadriennal du processus démocratique', *L'Afrique politique*.

* Obotela, Rashidi, 1992, 'Problèmatique des rôles électoraux au Zaïre', *Zaïre-Afrique*, 262, pp. 85-95.

Ohlson, T. and Stedman, S. J., 1994, *The New is Not Yet Born. Conflict Resolution in Southern Africa*, Washington DC, The Brookings Institution, 322p.

* Okamba, E., 1993, 'Analyse systémique des conférences nationales', *Afrique 2000*, 15, octobre-décembre, p. 21-38.

* Okbazghi, Y., 1993, 'Eritrea: A Country in Transition', *Review of African Political Economy*, 57, pp. 7-28.

Okigbo, C., 1992, 'Horse Race and Issues in Nigerian Elections', *Journal of Black Studies*, 22 (3), March, p. 349-365.

* Okoroji, J., 1993, 'The Nigerian Presidential Elections', *Review of African Political Economy*, 58, November, p. 123-130.

Okoth-Ogendo, H. W. O., 1993, 'Human and Peoples Rights: What Point is Africa Trying to Make', pp. 74-86, in Cohen R., Hyden G., *et al.* (eds.) *Human Rights and Governance in Africa*, Gainesville, Ed. Florida University Press, 312 p.

Olagunju, T., 1993, *Transition to Democracy in Nigeria (1985-1993)*, Ibadan, Safari Books.

Olaitan, W. A., 1992, 'Democracy and Democratization in Africa: Not Yet the Glorious Dawn', 423-434, in Caron B. Gboyega A. and Osaghae E. (eds.)*Democratic Transition in Africa*, Ibadan, CREDU, Proceedings of a Symposium, 436 p.

Olowu, D., 1992-93, 'Roots and Remedies of Governmental Corruption in Africa', *Corruption and Reform*, 7 (3), pp. 227-236.

* Omara-Otunnu, A., 1992, 'The Struggle for Democracy in Uganda', *Journal of Modern African Studies*, 30 (3), September, pp. 443-465.

Omoruyi, O., (ed.), 1992, *Grassroots Democracy and the New Local Government System in Nigeria*, Bwari, Centre for Democratic Studies.

Onana, H. F.,1994, *Les transitions démocratiques en Afrique: le cas du Cameroun*, Yaoundé.

* Osaghae, Eghosa, E., 1991, 'Babangida's Unique Transition Process in Nigeria and the Prospects', *Revue juridique africaine*, Nos. 2-3, pp.95-110.

* Osia, K., 1992, 'Leadership and Followership: Nigeria's Problem of Governance', *Scandinavian Journal of Development Alternatives*, 11 (3-4), septembre-décembre, pp.175-194.

Otayek, R., 1992, 'La rectification démocratique au Burkina Faso', *Studia Africanan*, 3, pp.11-26.

* Othman Haroub; Bavu Immanuel, K.; Okema Michael, (ed.), 1990, *Tanzania: Democracy in Transition*. Dar-es-Salaam, Dar-es-Salaam University Press, XI-244p.

Otlbogile, B., 1994, 'Judicial Intervention in the Election Process: The Botswana's Experience', *The Comparative and International Law Journal of Southern Africa*, 25 (2), July, (222-233).

* Otlhogile, B., 'How Free and Fair ?', pp. 23-28, Harare, SAPES, *State and Democracy*, 2, in Molomo M.G. and Mokopakgosi B.T. (eds.) *Multi-Party Democracy in Botswana 1991*, 63 p.

71

* Ottaway, Marina, 1991, 'Liberation Movements and Transition to Democracy: The Case of the ANC', (Examines Obstacles to Democracy in South Africa Arising out of Difficulties Experienced by ANC in Transforming itself from a Liberation Movement to a Political Party) *Journal of Modern African Studies*, 29 March, (61-82).

Ould Cheikh, A. W., 1994, 'Des voix dans le désert. Sur les élections de l'ère pluraliste', *Politique africaine*, 55, octobre: *La Mauritanie: Un tournant démocratique*, (31-39).

* Owusu, D. M., 1992, 'Democracy and Africa: A View from the Village', *Journal of Modern African Studies*, 30 (3), September.

* Oyediran, O., 1991, 'Two-Partyism and Democratic Transition in Nigeria', *Journal of Modern African Studies*, 29 (2), June, (213-235).

Oyono, D., 1991, 'Du parti unique au multipartisme: environment international et processus de démocratisation en Afrique', *Afrique 2000*, 6 August, (45-54).

Panter-Brick, K., 1994, 'Prospects for Democracy in Zambia', *Government and Opposition*, 29 (2), Spring, p. 231-247.

* Pazzanita, A. G., 1991, 'The Conflict Resolution Process in Angola', *Journal of Modern African Studies*, 29 (1), March, (83-114).

Pereira, A. W., 1994, 'The Neglected Tragedy: The Return to War in Angola 1992-1993', *Journal of Modern African Studies*, 32 (1), (1-28).

Perennes, J. J. and Puel, H., 1991, 'Démocratie et développement au sud', *Economie et Humanisme, 319*, décembre, (11-19).

Peterson, D., 1994, 'Debunking Ten Myths About Democracy in Africa', *Washington Quarterly*, 17 (3), Summer, (129-141).

* Philippe, C., 1991, 'Congo: l'expérience de la Conférence Nationale', *Défense nationale*, 47, novembre, (115-126).

* Philippe, Christine, 1992, 'La démocratie au Congo: La transition difficile', *Défense nationale: Etudes politiques, stratégies militaires, économiques et scientifiques* No. 5, mai, (43-56).

* Pilon, M., 1993, 'La transition togolaise dans l'impasse', *Politique africaine*, 49, mars, (136-140).

Pilon, M., 1994, 'L'observation des processus électoraux: enseignements de l'élection présidentielle du Togo', *Politique africaine*, 56, décembre, (137-143).

Pimont, Y., 1993, 'La constitution de la République du Mali', *Revue juridique et politique, indépendance et coopération*, 47 (3), septembre, (462-474).

Plurial Societies, 1992, 'South Africa', Special Issue, 22 (1-2), November, p. 248.

Pochon, J. F., 1992, 'Ajustement et démocratisation: l'atypisme du Gabon', *Géopolitique africaine*, 15 (1), janvier-février, (59-70).

Poithy, A., 1992, 'Problématique de la transition démocratique au Congo', *Géopolitique africaine*, 15 (1), janvier-février, (75-79).

Politique Africaine, 1992, 'Demokrasia ni nini? Fragments swahili du débat politique en Tanzanie', *Politique africaine* 47, (109-134).

Pollard, R.,1992-93, 'La démocratie ambiguë', *Année africaine*, (17-57).

Pondi, J. E. and Kuper, K., 1995, 'From Pariah to Pedagogue: South Africa's Contribution to Democracy in Africa', *SAIS Review*, 15 (1), Winter-Spring, (37-54).

Porteilla, R., 1992-93, 'La réintégration des TBVC en Afrique du sud: implications politiques et constitutionnelles', *Année africaine*, (215-242).

Posner, D. N., 1995, 'Malawi's New Dawn', *Journal of Democracy,* 6 (1), January, (131-145).

Pourgerami, A., 1991, *Development and Democracy in the Third World,* Boulder, Westview Press, 210 p.

Prunier, G., 'Le communisme est-il soluble dans l'ethnicité ?' *Relations internationales et stratégiques,* 14, Summer, pp.122-131.

* Pycroft, C., 1994, 'Angola: The Forgotten', *Journal of Southern African Studies,* 20 (2), June, pp. 241-262

* Qadir, S.; Clapham, C.; and Gills, B., 1993, 'Sustainable Democracy: Formalism vs Substance', *Third World Quaterly,* 14 (3), p. 415-422.

Quantin, P., 1989, 'Les élections générales de 1990 au Zimbabwe: vers le parti unique?', *Année africaine,* pp.165-188.

* Quantin, P., 1991, 'Zimbabwe: Perestroïka sans glasnost', *Politique africaine,* 44, décembre.

Quantin, P., 1994, 'Congo: les origines politiques de la décomposition d'un processus de libéralisation, August 1992-décembre 1993', *L'Afrique politique. Vue sur la démocratisation à marée basse,* pp. 167-190.

* Raftopoulos, B., 1992, 'Beyond the House of Hunger: Democratic Struggle in Zimbabwe', *Review of African Political Economy,* 55, November, pp. 57-66.

Rai, S. M., 1994, 'Gender and Democratization: or What Does Democracy Mean for Women in the Third Word?', *Democratization,* 1(2), Summer, 1994, pp. 209-228.

* Raison, J. P., 1993, 'Une esquisse de géographie électorale malgache', *Politique africaine,* 52, décembre, *Madagascar,* pp. 67-75.

* Raison-Jourde, F., 1993, 'Une transition achevée ou amorcée?', *Politique africaine,* 52, Decembre, *Madagascar,* pp. 6-18.

Rakner, L. G., 1992, *Trade Unions in Process of Democratization: a Study of Party Labour Relations in Zambia,* Bergen, Chr. Michelsen Institute, Report 6, 177 p.

Rakontondrable, D. T., 1993, 'Beyond the Ethnic Group: Ethnic Groups, Nation State and Democracy in Madagascar', *Transformation,* 22.

* Ramamonjisoa, S., 1993, 'Empowerment of Women and Democracy in Madagascar', *Review of African Political Economy,* 58, November, pp. 118-123.

Ramose, M. B., 1992, 'African Democratic Tradition: Oneness, Consensus and Openess: A Reply to Wamba-dia-Wamba', *Quest,* 6 (2), pp. 62-83.

* Randall, V., 1993, 'The Media and Democratization in the Third World', *Third World Quarterly,* 14 (3), pp. 625-646.

Ranger, T. and Vaughan, O. (eds.), 1993, *Legitimacy and the State in the Twentieth Century Africa,* London, Macmillan, 210 p.

* Rantete Johannes; Giliomee Hermann, 1992, 'Transition to Democracy Through Transaction ? Bilateral Negotiations Between the ANC and NP in South Africa', *African Affairs,* Vol. 91, No. 365, October, pp.515-542

* Ravaloson, J., 1993, 'Madagascar: la révolution tranquille', *Afrique 2000,* 15, Octobre-décembre, pp.139-154.

Ravaloson, Jaona., 1994, *Transition démocratique à Madagascar,* Paris, l'Harmattan, 175 p.

* Raynal, J. J., 1993, 'La constitution nigérienne du 26 décembre 1992', *Afrique contemporaine,* 165, 1st Quarter.

Raynal, J. J., 1994, 'Les conférences nationales en Afrique: au-delà du mythe, la démocratie?' *Penant,* 104 (86), octobre-décembre.

* Razafindratandra, Y., 1993, 'Mission d'observation du second tour des élections présidentielles à Madagascar', *Politique africaine,* 52, décembre, *Madagascar,* pp. 89-101.

Reddy, P. S., 1993, 'Local Government in Transition for a Democratic South Africa', *Politeïa,* 12 (1), pp. 39-50.

* Reno, W., 1993, 'Old Brigades, Money Bags, New Breeds, and the Ironies of Reform in Nigeria. Canadian', *Journal of African Studies,* 27 (1), pp. 66-87.

Repnik, H. P. and Mohs, R. M., 1992, 'Good Governance, Democracy and Development Paradigms', *Intereconomics,* 27 (1), January, pp. 28-33.

Revel, J. F, 1991, *Le regain démocratique,* Paris, Fayart, 522 p.

Reynolos, A., 1994, *Election '94 South Africa: The Campaign, Results and Future Prospects* London, James Currey.

Reyntjens, F., 1991, 'The Winds of Change. Political and Constitutionnal Evolution in Francophone Africa, 1990-1991', *Journal of African Law,* 35 (1-2), pp.44-55.

* Reyntjens, F., 1992, 'L'ingénierie de l'unité nationale: quelques singularités de la constitution burundaise de 1992', *Politique africaine,* 47, octobre, pp. 141-146.

* Reyntjens, F., 1993, 'The Proof of the Pudding is in the Eating: The June 1993 Elections in Burundi', *Journal of Modern African Studies,* 31 (4), December, 563-584).

Reyntjens, P., 1993, 'Démocratisation et conflits ethniques au Rwanda et au Burundi', *Cahiers africains,* 4-5, (209-227).

Rifrac, S., 1992, 'De La Baule à Libreville. De la démocratie à la gestion rigoureuse', *Cahiers du communisme,* 68 (11), novembre.

Rigaux, F., 1992, 'Impératif démocratique et droit international', *Trimestre du monde,* 17, 1er trimestre, (37-51).

* Rijnierse, E., 1993, 'Democratization in Africa? Literature Overview', *Third World Quarterly* 14 (3), (647-664).

* Riley, Stephen P., 1992, 'Political Adjustment or Domestic Pressure: Democratic Politics and Political Choice in Africa', *Third World Quarterly* 13 (3), (539-51).

* Riley, S. P., 1992-93, 'Post Independence Anti-Corruption Strategies and the Contemporary Effects of Democratization', *Corruption and Reform* 7 (3), (249-261).

Robertson, P., 1994, 'Monitoring African Elections', in Rimmer D. (ed.) *Action in Africa: The Experience of People in Government Business and Aid,* London, Portsmouth, James Currey, Heinemann, (154-157).

* Robinson, M., 1993, 'Aid, Democracy and Political Conditionality in Sub-Saharan Africa', *European Journal of Development Research,* 5 (1), juin.

* Robinson, M., 1993, «Will Political Conditionality Work?', IDS Bulletin, 24 (1), (58-66).

Robinson, P. T., 1991, 'Niger: An Anatomy of Neotraditionnal Corporatist State', *Comparative Politics,* 24 (1), October, (1-20).

Robinson, P. T., 1994a, 'The National Conference Phenomenon in Francophone Africa', *Comparative Studies in Society and History,* 36 (3), July, (575-610).

Robinson, P. T., 1994b, 'Democratization: Understanding the Relationship Between Regime Change and the Culture of Politics', *The African Studies Review,* 37 (1), April, (39-68).

* Rossatanga-Rignault, G., 1993, 'Les partis politiques gabonais: un essai d'analyse', *Afrique 2000*, 14, juillet-septembre.

* Rossatanga-Rignault, G., 1993, 'L'insoutenable condition du clerc gabonais',*Politique Africaine*, 51, octobre.

Rossatanga-Rignault, G., 1993, 'Faut-il avoir peur des Fang ? De la démocratisation and de l'ethnisme au Gabon', *Droit et Cultures*, 26.

Rothstein, R. L., 1992, 'Democracy Conflict and Development in the Third World', *Washington Quaterly*, 14 (2), (43-63).

Roussillon, Henry, 1992, *Les Nouvelles constitutions africaines: la transition démocratique* Toulouse, Presses de l'Institut d'études politiques, 191 p.

Roy, M. P., 1992, 'Le Bénin: un modèle de sortie de dictature et de transition démocratique en Afrique noire', *Revue de la recherche juridique, Droit prospectif* 17, (50), 3ème trimestre, (585-604).

* Sabar-Friedman, G., 1995, 'The Mau Mau Myth: Kenyan Political Discourse in Search of Democracy', *Cahiers d'études africaines*, 35 (1), pp. 101-132.

* Saint Moulin, L. D., et Umba Di, Mambuku, 1993 'Le mouvement de démocratisation dans la zone de Ngaba à Kinshasa', *Zaïre-Afrique*, 274, (225-243).

Sakamoto, Y., 1991, 'The Global Contexte of Democratization',*Alternatives*, no. spécial, 16 (2), Spring, (119-128).

Sakhela, Maree Johann, Cherry Janet, Haines Richard, Klerck Gilton, 1995,*Taking Democracy Seriously: Worker Expectations and Parliamentary Democracy in South Africa*, Durban, Indicator Press, April, 114p.

Sall, E., 1995, 'Gambie: le coup d'Etat de juillet 1994',*L'Afrique Politique*.

Sanbrook, R., 1993, *The Politics of Africa's Economic Recovery*. Cambridge, Cambridge University Press, 1993, 170 p.

Saul, J. S.,1994, 'Globalism, Socialism and Democracy in the South African Transition', *Socialist Register*, (171-201).

Sawadogo, J. M., 1990, 'La démocratie africaine hypothéquée ?' *Echanges et Projets*, 62, La démocratisation en Afrique, décembre, (33-37).

Sayena, S. C., 1992-93 'Nation Building in South Africa: Agenda for the Future',*Africa Quaterly*, 32 (1-4), (91-106).

* Schatzberg, M. G., 1993, 'Power, Legitimacy and Democratization in Africa', Africa, 63 (4), (445-461).

Schifter, R., 1994, 'Is There a Democracy Gene?' *Washington Quarterly*, 17 (3), été, (121-127).

* Schraeder, P. J., 1994, 'Elites as Facilitators or Impediments to Political Development ? Some Lessons from the Third Wave of Democratization in Africa', *The Journal of Developing Areas*, 29 (1), October, (69-89).

Seck, P. L., 1990, 'La perspective démocratique en Afrique', *Echanges et Projets*, 62, La démocratisation en Afrique, décembre, pp. 39-45.

* Shilder, K., 1993, 'La démocratie aux champs, les présidentielles d'octobre au nord-Cameroun', *Politique africaine*, 50, juin, pp. 115-121.

Shillington, K., 1992, *Ghana and the Rawlings Factor*, London, Macmillan, 184p.

Shin, D. C., 1994, 'On the Third Wave of Democratization: A Synthesis and Evaluation of Recent Theory and Research', *World Politics*, 47 (1), October.

Shivji, I. J., 1988, *Fight my Beloved Continent New Democracy in Africa*, Harare, SAPES, 40p.

* Shivji, I. J. (ed.), 1991, *State and Constitutionalism: An African Debate on Democracy* Harare, SAPES, 287 p.

Shubane, K., 1992, 'Civil Society in Apartheid and Post-Apartheid South Africa',*Theoria*, 79, (33-41).

* Sidaway, J. D. and Simon, D., 1993, 'Geopolitical Transition and State Formation: The Changing Political Geographies of Angola, Mozambique and Namibia', Journal of Southern African Studies, 19 (1), (6-28).

Siddiqui, R. A., 1993, *Sub-Saharan Africa: A Sub-Continent in Transition, Avebury,*368 p.

* Simone, A. M. and Pieterse, E., 1993, 'Civil Societies in Internationalized Africa', *Social Dynamics*, 19 (2), (41-49).

Sindjoun, L., 1990-93, 'Cameroun: Le système politique face aux enjeux de la transition démocratique', *L'Afrique politique*, 1994: *Vue sur la démocratisation à marée basse*, (143-166).

Sindjoun, L., 1994, 'Dynamiques de civilisation de l'Etat et de production du politique baroque en Afrique noire', *Verfassung und Recht in übersee*, 27 (2), 2ème trimestre, (191-230).

Sithole, M., 1993, 'Is Zimbabwe Posed on a Liberal Path ?' *Issue*, 21 (1-2),: *Toward a new African Political Order, African Perspectives on Democratization Process, Regional Conflict Management*, (35-43).

Sklar, R. L. and Strege, M., 1992, 'Finding Peace Through Democracy in Sahelian Africa', *Current History*, 91 (565), May.

Slabbert, Frederik van Zyl, 1992, *Quest for Democracy: South African in Transition*, Longman Penguin Southern Africa (Pty) Ltd.,107 p.

Smith, D. M., 1992, 'Redistribution After Apartheid: Who Gets What Where in the New South Africa', *Adrea*, 24 (4), 1992, (350-358).

Somerville, K., 1993, 'The Failure of Democratic Reform in Angola and Zaïre', Survival, 35 (3), Autumn (51-77).

* Southall, R., Segar, J. and Donaldson, A., 1992, 'A Transkei Beyond the Transition Towards Good Government or Back to the Frontier?' *Journal of Contemporay African Studies*, 11 (2), (270-279).

* Southall, R., 1994, 'The 1993 Lesotho Elections', *Review of African Political Economy*, 59, March.

Southall, R., 1994, 'The South African Election of 1994: The Remaking of the Dominant Party-State', *Journal of Modern African Studies*, 32 (4), December, (629-656).

Spence, J. E., 1993 'A Post Apartheid South Africa and the International Community', *Journal of Commonwealth and Comparative Politics*, 31 (3), (84-95).

Spence, J. E., 1994, 'Comment: Reflections of a First Time Voter', *African Affairs*, 93 (372), July, (341-342).

Stadler, A. W., 1989, 'Les conditions de la démocratie dans l'Afrique du Sud de demain', *Année Africaine*, (37-60).

Stepan, A. and Skach, C., 1993, 'Constitutionnal Frameworks and Democratic Consolidation, Parliamentarism vs Presidentialism', *World Politics*, 46 (1), October, (1-24).

* Strauss, A., 1993, 'The 1992 Referendum in South Africa', *Journal of Modern African Studies*, 31 (2), (339-360).

Susungi, N. N., 1992, *The Crisis of Unity and Democracy in Cameroon: Can a Country Which as Pronounced Itself Dead Be Saved By Democracy?* s.l., s.n., 349 p.

* Swilling, M., 1990, 'Political Transition Development and the Role of Civil Society', *Africa Insight*, 20 (3), (151-160).

Swilling, M., 1992, 'Quixote at the Windsmills, Another Conspiracy Thesis from Steven Friedman', *Theoria*, 79, (97-104).

Swilling M., 1992, 'Socialism, Democracy and Civil Society: the Case for Associational Socialism', *Theoria*, 79, (75-82).

Swing, W. L., 1991, *Peacemaking and Democracy in Southern Africa: An American View*, Johannesburg, SAIIA, Occasional Paper, 10 p.

* Szeftel, M., 1994, 'Ethnicity and Democratization in South Africa', *Review of African Political Economy*, 21 (60), June, (185-199).

Tabapssi, F. T., 1993, 'Les conditions socio-économiques de la démocratisation and de la démocratie', in *Democracy and Democratization in Africa, The Hague, Institute of Social Studies/Global Coalition for Africa*, Final Report, 5 April, (106-114).

* Tall, E. K., 1995, 'De la démocratie et des cultes vaudous au Bénin', *Cahiers d'Etudes Africaines*, 35 (1), pp. 195-209.

Tavernier, P., 1994, 'Les Nations Unies et la question de l'Afrique du Sud', *Revue juridique et politique, indépendance et coopération*, 1, janvier-mars 1994, (27-45).

Tegegn, M., 1993, 'Beyond Accountability and Rights: Some Remarks on the Process of Democratizaton in Africa with Focus on Post-Mengistu Ethiopia', in *Democracy and Democratization in Africa* The Hague, Institute of Social Studies/Global Coalition for Africa, Final Report, 5 April, (46-52).

Thassinda, Uba Thassinda, 1992, *Zaïre: les princes de l'invisible, l'Afrique noire baillonnée par le parti unique.* Caen, C'est-à-dire, 423 p.

* Throup, D., 1993, 'Elections and Political Legitimacy in Kenya', *Africa*, 63 (4), *Understanding Elections in Africa*, (371-396).

Thystere-Tchicaya, J. P., 1992, *Itinéraire d'un africain vers la démocratie*, Genève, Tricorne, 171 p.

* Tiangaye, N., 1992, 'Aux sources du pluralisme politique en Afrique', *Afrique 2000*, 11, novembre, (55-66).

Titra Liberties, 1993, *Les conférences nationales africaines dans la presse*, Paris, AIPLF-PARDOC, non paginé p.

Tomkys, R., 1994, 'Implementing Africa's Second Liberation. The Case of Kenya', in Rimmer D. (ed.), *Action in Africa: The Experience of People in Government Business and Aid.* London, Portsmouth, James Currey, Heinemann, (144-153).

* Topanou, K. V., 1994, 'De la démocratie en Afrique', *Afrique 2000*, 19, octobre-décembre, (53-59).

Tordoff, W., 1994, 'Political Liberalization and Economic Reform in Africa', *Democratization*, 1 (1), Spring, (100-115).

Tordoff, W., 1994, 'Decentralization: Comparative Experience in Commonwealth Africa', *Journal of Modern African Studies*, 32 (4), December, (555-580).

Torres, L., 1995, 'South African Unions: Schools or Agents for Democracy', *Journal of Contemporary African Studies*, 13 (1), January, (35-55).

Tostensen, A., 1993, 'The Ambiguity of Civil Society in the Democratization Process', in Ofstad A. & Wiig A. (eds.), *Development Theory: Recent Trends*

Toulabor, C., 1992, 'L'automne des Dictateurs', Belvédère, 4 (1294), janvier-février, (46-48).

Toulabor, C., 1993, 'Perestroïka et revendication démocratique', *in* Bach D.C. et Kirk-Greene A.H.M. (sous la direction), *Etats et sociétés en Afrique francophone, Paris, Economica*, (119-135).

Toulabor, C., 1993, 'La bataille finale du Général Eyadéma au Togo', *Le Monde Diplomatique*, mars.

Toulabor, C., 1994, 'Ghana: Nouvelles églises et processus de démocratisation', *L'Afrique Politique*: Vue sur la démocratisation à marée basse, (31-142).

Toulassi, V. K. et Alem, K. A., 1994, 'La presse libre au Togo: à quand la mutation ?', *Politique Africaine*, 54, juin, (160-162).

Tripp, A. M., 1992, «Local Organizations, Participation and the State in Urban Tanzania', in Hyden G. et Bratton M. (eds.), Governance and Politics in Africa. Boulder, Lynne Rienner Publishers, 329 p., (221-242).

Tshiyembe, M.; Bukasa, M., 1992, *Invention de l'Etat de droit et projet de société démocratique en Afrique: le cas du Zaïre*, Paris, Selliers, 220 p.

* Tshiyembe, M., 1993, 'Résistances actuelles à la démocratisation en Afrique', *Afrique 2000*, 14 juillet-septembre 1993, (39-48).

Tshosha, O. B., 1994, 'Freedom of Political Activity: Law and Practice in Botswana', *The Comparative and International Law Journal of Southern Africa*, 23 (3), November, (371-382).

* Tsie, B., 1991, 'Election Democracy and Hegemony in Botswana', in Molomo M.G. et Mokopakgosi B.T. (eds.), *Multi-Party Democracy in Botswana* Harare, SAPES, State and Democracy, 2, 63 p, (49-53).

Turok, B, (ed.), 1989, 1991, *Alternative Strategies for Africa*, London Institute for African Alternatives, Conférence de Dar-es-Salaam, 264 p.

* Udogu, E. Ike, 1994, 'Democracy in Two-Party System and the Transition Imbrogio in the March Toward Nigeria's Third Republic 1985-1992', *Scandinavian Journal of Development Alternatives*, Vol. 13, No. 1/2, March and June, (205-220).

Urfer, S., 1993, 'Quand les églises entrent en politique', *Politique Africaine*, 52, décembre, Madagascar, (31-39).

Uyanne, F. U, 1994, 'Intranational Boundaries and Democratization in Africa', in Democracy and Democratization in Africa. Enschede, International Institute for Aerospace Survey and Earth Science/Global Coalition for Africa. Final Report, 18-19 March, 92 p. (12-23).

Vahhaven, T., 1990, 'The Process of Democratization: A Comparative Study of 147 States, 1980-88', New York Crane Russak, 327p.

Van Binsbergen, W., 1995, 'Aspects of Democracy and Democratization in Zambia and Botswana: Exploring African Political Culture at the Grassroots', *Journal of Contemporary African Studies*, 13 (1), January, (3-34).

Van Cranenburgh, O., 1994, 'African Democratization: Contextual Factors and Institutional Choice', *Leidschrift*, 10 (2), June.

* Van Hoeck, F. J. et Bossuyt, J., 1993, 'Democracy in Subsaharan Africa: The Search for a New Institutionnal Set-Up', *African Development Review*, 5 (1), June, (81-93).

Van Nieuwerk, A., 1992, *Transitional Politics in South Africa: From Confrontation to Democracy?* Johannesburg, SAIIA, Occasional Paper, 38 p.

Van Vuuren, W., 1994, 'Transition Politics and Democracy as Good Governance', Africanus, 24 (1), (62-66).

* Van Wyk, M. J., 1993, 'Civil Society and Democracy in South Africa', *Africa Insight*, 23 (3), (136-140).

Van Zyl, S. F., 1992, 'Dilemmas for Democracy in South Africa', *South Africa International*, 23 (1), July, (4-10).

Van Zyl, S. F., 1992, *The Burden of Democracy*, Braamfontein, SAIIA, 13 p.

* Vengroff, R., 1993, 'Governance and the Transition to Democracy: Political Parties and the Party System in Mali', *Journal of Modern African Studies*, 31 (4), December 1993, (541-562).

Vengroff, R., 1994, 'The Impact of the Electoral System on the Transition to Democracy in Africa: the Case of Mali', *Electoral Studies*, 13 (1), (29-37).

* Vengwekhulu, R., 1991, 'The Electoral Process', in Molomo M.G. et Mokopakgosi B.T. (eds.), Multi-Party Democracy in Botswana, Harare, SAPES and Democracy, 2, 63 p, (39-47).

Vidal, C., 1995, 'Côte d'Ivoire: Funérailles présidentielles et dévaluation entre décembre1993 et mars 1994', L'Afrique politique.

* Vidyasekera, E. A., 1994, 'Glimpses on Transition from Apartheid', *Development and Socio-Economic Progress*, No. 59, January-June, (5-9).

Vieira, S., 1992, Moçambique: interrogaçoes sobre a emergencia da sociedade civile, Estudos Maçambicanos.

Viljoen, G., 1991, 'Multyparty Conference Paves the Way', *RSA Policy Review*, 4 (5), June, (3-17).

Villalon, L. A., 1994, 'Democratizing a (Quasi) Democracy: the Senegalese Elections of 1993', *African Affairs*, 93 (371), April, (163-194).

Vines, A. et Wilson, K., 1993, *Churches and Peace Process in Mozambique: The Christian Churches and Africa's Democratization*, University of Leeds, Conference 20-23 September.

Vittin, T. E., 1992, 'Crise, renouveau démocratique et mutation du paysage médiatique au Bénin', Afrique 2000, 9, (37-57).

* Volman, D., 1993, 'Africa and the New World Order', Journal of Modern African Studies, 31 (1), March (1-30).

* Von Trotha, Dr T., 1993, 'C'est la pagaille: Remarques sur l'élection présidentielle au Togo', Politique Africaine, 52, décembre, (152-159).

Vusani, C. Z., 1993, 'The Democratization Process in Africa', in Democracy and Democratization in Africa, The Hague, Institute of Social Studies/Global Coalition for Africa, Final Report, 5 April, (72-88).

Wagao, J. H., 1993, 'Multi-Partism and the Tanzanian Economy: Some Challenges', in Bagachwa M.S.D. et Mbelle A.V.Y. (eds.), Economic Policy under a Multiparty System in Tanzania. Dar-es-Salaam, Dar-es-Salaam Universiy Press, (125-140).

Waligoo, J. M., 1994, 'Le Développement de la démocratie en Afrique', *Zaïre-Afrique*, 34 (283), mars, pp. 133-142.

Wamba-dia-Wamba, E., 1992, 'Beyond Elite Politics of Democracy in Africa', *Quest*, 6 (1), (28-42).

* Wamba-dia-Wamba, E., 1993, 'Democracy Multipartyism and Emancipative Politics in Africa, The Case of Zaïre', *Africa Development*, 18 (4),

Weiland, H., 1991, 'Democratic Spring in Africa? The Demise of the One-Party State?' *International Affairs Bulletin*, 15 (2), (5-22).

Weiland, H., 1992, 'Demokratie und Nationale Entwicklung in Namibia: eine Zwischenbilanz nach Zweieinhalb Jahren Unabhängigkeit', *Africa Spectrum*, 3, (273-301).

Weissman, F., 1994, L'élection présidentielle de 1992 au Congo: entreprise politique et mobilisation partisane. Bordeaux, CEAN, 138 p.

Welch, C., 1992, 'Military Disengagement from Politics, Paradigms, Process and Random Events', *Armed Forces and Societies*, 18 (3), Spring, (323-342).

* Wells, M., 1993, 'Namibie: la constitution du 21 mars 1990', *Afrique Contemporaine*, 167, 3ème trimestre, (45-84).

White, G., 1994, 'Civil Society, Democratization and Development (1): Clearing the Analytical Ground', Democratization, 1 (3), Autumn, (375-390).

Widner, J. A., 1994, 'Two Leadership Styles and Patterns of Political Liberalization', *The African Studies Review*, 37 (1), April.

Willame, J. C. 1991, 'Zaïre années 90. De la démocratie octroyée à la démocratie enrayée'.

Willame, J. C., 1992, 'Les manipulations du développement: ajustement, cogestion et démocratisation au Burundi', Bruxelles, CEDAF, *Les cahiers du CEDAF*, 5, 182p.

Willame, J. C., 1993, 'Allez et démocratiser toutes les nations', *Revue Nouvelle*, 86 (1-2), janvier-février, (113-121).

* Williams, D. C., 1992, 'Assessing Future Democracy Accountability in Nigeria: Investigative Tribunals and Nigerian Political Culture', *Scandinavian Journal of Development Alternatives*, 11 (3-4), (51-65).

Windrich, E., 1994, 'Media Coverage of the Angola Elections', *Issue*, 22 (1), Winter/Spring, (19-23).

Winsome, L., 1993, *Zaïre: Certainty and Political Change in an Oppressive State*, Boulder, Westview Press.

* Wiseman, J. A., 1991, 'Democratic Resurgence in Black Africa', *Contemporary Review*, 259 (1506), July, (7-13).

Wiseman, J. A., 1992, 'Early Post-Redemocratization Elections in Africa', *Electoral Studies*, 11 (4), (279-291).

* Wiseman, J. A., 1993, 'Democracy and the New Political Pluralism in Africa: Causes, Consequences and Significance', *Third World Quarterly*, 14 (3), (439-450).

* Wiseman, J. A., 1993, 'Leadership and Personal Danger in African Politics', *Journal of Modern African Studies*, 31 (4), (657-660).

Wolfgang, Marvin, E. (ed.), 1997, *Africa in Transition*, American Academy of Political & Social Science.

Wonyu, E., 1990, 'Les jeunes et l'exigence d'un nouvel ordre politique en Afrique', *Afrique 2000*, 3, novembre, (67-76).

80

* Woods, D., 1992, 'Civil Society in Europe and Africa: Limiting State Power Through a Public Sphere', *The African Studies Review*, 35 (2), (77-100).

Woodward, P., 1994, 'Democracy and Economy in Africa: The Optimists and the Pessimists', *Democratization*, 1(1), Spring, (116-132).

Yabouet-Bazoly, S., 1990, 'Inventer le citoyen en Afrique noire?', *Histoires de Développement*, 9, mai (33-35).

Yakemtchouck, R., 1991, 'Une démocratie pour l'Afrique', *Studia Diplomatica*, no. spécial, 44 (2), (5-126).

Yonaba, S., 1993, 'La Conférence Nationale et le droit: les leçons de l'expérience burkinabé', *Revue juridique et politique*, 1, janvier-mars, (78-108).

* Zaffiro, J. J, 1993, 'Mass Media, Politics and Society in Botswana: The 1990's and Beyond', *Africa Today*, 40 (1), *Botswana, Achievements and Challenges*, (7-25).

Zaïre-Afrique, 1993, 'Rapport final des travaux de la Conférence nationale souveraine', *Zaïre-Afrique*, 273, mars.

Section 4: Latin America

Farcau, Bruce, W., 1996, *The Transition To Democracy in Latin America: The Role of the Military*, Greenwood Publishing Group, Incorporated.

* Jaquette, Jane, S., 1989, (ed.), *The Women's Movement in Latin America: Feminism and the Transition to Democracy*, London, Unwin Hyman, 215p.

Malloy, James, M., (ed.), 1987, *Authoritarians and Democrats: Regime Transition in Latin America*, University of Pittsburgh Press, 288 p.

Morales, Juan, 1996, *Economic Policy and the Transition to Democracy: Latin American Experience*, London, Macmillan Business.

Munck, Ronaldo, 1985, 'On Negotiating Democratic Transition', Third World Quaterly, 7 April, (vii-xvi).

* Munck, Ronaldo, 1989, *Latin America: The Transition to Democracy*, London, Zed Books, 212p.

O'Donnell, Guillermo (ed.), 1986, *Transitions From Authoritarian Rule: Latin America*, Johns Hopkins University Press, 272 p.

Skidmore, Thomas, E., (ed.), 1993, *Television, Politics, and the Transition to Democracy in Latin America*, Wilson Centre Press, U.S., 168 p.

Stotzky, Irwin, P., (ed.), 1993, *Transition to Democracy in Latin America: The Role of the Judiciary*, Boulder, Westview Press, 403 p.

Tulchin, Joseph; Varas, Augusto (ed.), 1991, *From Dictatorship to Democracy: Rebuilding Political Consensus in Chile*, Boulder, Lynne Rienner Publishers, viii, 91 p.

Section 5: Asia

Alagappa, Muthiah, 1994, *Democratic Transition in Asia: The Role of the International Community*, DIANE Publishing Company, 51 p.

Bahadur, Kalim (ed.), 1989, *Pakistan Transition to Democracy: Joint Study of Indian and Pakistani Scholars*, South Asia Books.

Bernstorff, Dagmar (ed.), 1991, *Political Transition in South Asia*, Franz Steiner Verlag Stuttgart, xvi, 168 p.

Brown, Louise, 1996, *Transition to Democracy in Nepal*, Routledge, 232 p.

Ethier, Diane, 1990, *Democratic Transition and Consolidation in Southern Europe, Latin America and South-east Asia*, International Political Economy Series.

Friedman, Edward (ed.), 1994, *Politics of Democratization*, Boulder, Westview Press Inc., US.

Leng, Tse-Kang, 1996, *The Taiwan-China Economic Connection: Democracy and Development Across the Taiwan Straits*, Boulder, Westview Press.

OECD Staff, 1994, *From Reform to Growth: China and Other Countries in Transition in Asia and Central and Eastern Europe*, OECD, 286 p.

Ross, Robert, S., (ed.), 1995, *East Asia in Transition: Toward a New Regional Order*, May/ 392 p., Sharpe (M. E.) Inc., U.S.

Rumer, Boris, 1996, *Central Asia in Transition: Dilemma of Political and Economic Development*, Sharpe (M. E.) Inc., U.S., 320 p.

Saxena, Rekha, 1994, *Indian Politics in Transition: From Dominance to Chaos*, South Asia Books.

Section 6: Eastern Europe

Berglund, Sten, (ed.), 1994, *The New Democracies in Eastern Europe: Party Systems and Political Cleavages*, Ashgate Publishing Company, 272 p.

Beyme, Klaus, 1996, *Transition to Democracy in Eastern Europe*, Macmillan Business.

Blanchard, Jean, O., (ed.), 1994, *The Transition in Eastern Europe: Restructuring* University of Chicago Press, 384 p.

* Campeanu, Pavel, 'Transition in Eastern Europe', 1990, *Social Research*, Vol. 57, No. 3, (587-530).

Cowen-Karp, Regina, (ed.), 1994, *Central and Eastern Europe: The Challenge of Transition*, Oxford University Press, Incorporated, 336 p.

Derlien, Hans-Ulrich, 1993, *Regimes Transitions, Elites and Bureaucracies in Eastern Europe*, Blackwell (Basil) Inc., U.S.

* Gati, Charles, 1990, *The Bloc That Failed: Soviet-East European Relations in Transition*, Indiana University Press, 242 p.

Gazdag, Ferenc, 1993, *Problems of Transition: From Communism to Democracy* Kent State University, Lyman L. Lemnitzer Center for NATO and European Community Studies.

Institut International d'Administration Publique (France), 1992, *L'Etat en transition. L'Europe centrale.* Institut international d'administration publique, Paris, IIAP, en annexe, constitutions de la République de Bulgarie et de la Roumanie. Publié à l'occasion de la Table ronde organisée le 20 novembre 1991 pour le XXVe anniversaire de l'IIAP.

International Conference on World Politics Staff, *Eastern Europe in Transition*, Papers, REP (ed.), Books on Demand, (Date Not Supplied), 386 p.

Karvonen, Lauri, 1991, *Social Democracy in Transition: Northern, Southern and Eastern Europe*, Ashgate Publishing Company, 332 p.

Menges, Constantine, C., (ed.), 1993, *Transitions from Communism in Russia and Eastern Europe: Analysis and Perspectives*, University Press of America, 320p.

Mey, Jacob, L.,1996, *Political Discourse in Transition in Eastern and Western Europe 1989-1991*, John Benjamins North America, Incorporated, 300 p.

Pravda, Alex, 1992, *The End of the Other Empire: Soviet Union - East European Relations in Transition*, Sage Publications, 256 p.

Pridham, Geoffrey, (ed.), 1995, *Transitions to Democracy: Comparative Perspectives from Southern Europe, Latin America and Eastern Europe*, Ashgate Publishing Company.

Remington, (ed.), 1995, *Parliaments in Transition: The New Legislative Politics in the Former U.S.S.R. and Eastern Europe*, Westview Press Inc., U.S.

Von, Beyme, (s.d.), *The Transition to Democracy in Eastern Europe*, Saint Martin's Press, Incorporated.

Wightman, Gordon, (ed.), 1995, *Party Formation in East-Central Europe: Post-Communist Politics in Czechoslovakia, Hungary, Poland & Bulgaria*, Ashgate Publishing Company, 296 p.

Williams, Shirley, 1992, *The Agony of Transition: from Communism to Democracy, Problems of Transition in Societies of Eastern Europe - Socioeconomic and Political Perspectives; Outlines Areas of Western Intervention to Aid Process*, RSA J. 140 (May), (369-79).

Zagorska, Janina, 1993, *From a One-party State to Democracy: Transition in Eastern Europe*, Rodopi B. V. Editions, Amsterdam.

Achevé d'imprimer
sur les presses de l'Imprimerie Saint-Paul
Angle rues El Hadj Mbaye Guèye (ex Sandiniéry) / Dr Thèze
D A K A R
Juin 1998

www.ingramcontent.com/pod-product-compliance
Lightning Source LLC
Chambersburg PA
CBHW020007290326
41935CB00007B/336